Praise for *Raising L*

An important read for educators, parents, and anyone who cares about helping our youth navigate the digital world and become digitally savvy, civil, and safe.

—Barbara Coloroso, educator and author of
The Bully, the Bullied, and the Not-So-Innocent Bystander
and *Kids Are Worth It!*

When I work with parents on children's use of social media, I always focus on these two things: how do we ensure the safety of our children, and how do we open up every door for them to be successful in our world today? Jennifer Casa-Todd addresses these questions and discusses the ins and outs of technology with children and parents. She also leaves lots of room for families to make the best decisions for their own children when it comes to technology use. I appreciate her approach, which makes this book conversational, full of information, and free from judgment.

—George Couros, educator and author of
The Innovator's Mindset* and *Innovate Inside the Box

This book is a must-read for every parent! As a mom, educator, and researcher, Jennifer Casa-Todd addresses common fears about young adolescents and technology, and she helped me put my hopes and fears into perspective. This book is full of strategies for engaging in productive conversations about technology and social media, and it will help you understand how you can raise confident and successful digital leaders.

—Katie Martin, mom, educator, and author of
Learner-Centered Innovation

Raising Digital Leaders is exactly what we need right now. My husband and I have been public school educators for over twenty-four years and have a fourteen-year-old daughter and a ten-year-old son. We try to encourage a healthy balance of screen-free activities and time for our children to use technology, but it hasn't been easy, especially now during COVID-19, with all of us forced to use technology and social media more than ever before. I personally love the straightforward information about what to expect and when to worry, as well as the tips for creating device-free times and zones. This book makes it easy to help us guide our children in creating a positive online presence and to protect them from fake and misleading news. Cyberbullying is addressed in a thoughtful, strategic way, which I appreciate. I highly recommend this book to all families.

—Jennifer Lee Quattrucci, author of *Educate the Heart* and creator and owner of mommyteacherfashionista.com, an education-based lifestyle blog

As a connected dad, I still wonder how I can make sure my boys are safe online and offline. As I read through Jennifer's experiences and researched tools and suggestions, I realized she was giving advice that needs to be shared with millions of other deeply concerned parents. She brings us back to the foundations of relationships and how to ensure their success and tips to strengthen them when they are out of balance. I connected to her heart-touching stories and determined to use the tools she outlines so clearly. When you read this book, do so with an open mind and heart to give the best to your growing and ever-changing children, knowing they look to you as a model for how to navigate life and its evolving challenges.

—Rodney Turner, father, educator, project manager

No one ever said parenting would be easy. Throw in the challenges of raising children in an ever-changing digital age and one might think it next to impossible. In her latest book, *Raising Digital Leaders*, Jennifer Casa-Todd offers up her invaluable expertise and insights as an educator, parent, speaker, and innovator, and she presents strategies to help parents support their children as they endeavor to find their places in the digital world. Each chapter focuses on important topics and addresses questions relating to the use of technology that so often torment parents or that we may feel too embarrassed to ask. In sharing research-based tips, inspirational examples of children leveraging social media to do good, and her firsthand experience with bullying, Jennifer will compel you with this book to check and connect with your own children, become empowered to be their media mentor, and who knows what else. It just may enable you to help them become the digital role models of tomorrow.

—Diana Mancuso, elementary French teacher, blogger, and edtech enthusiast

This comprehensive book shares all the latest research on kids and media and offers an experienced educator's perspective on questions like when to get kids a phone and how to teach them safer ways to use social media.

—Dr. Devorah Heitner, author of *Screenwise*

Raising Digital Leaders

Jennifer Casa-Todd

Raising Digital Leaders

Practical Advice for Families
Navigating Today's Technology

Raising Digital Leaders: Practical Advice for Families Navigating Today's Technology
©2021 Jennifer Casa-Todd

This book is available at special discounts when purchased in quantity for educational purposes or for use as premiums, promotions, or fundraisers. For inquiries and details, contact the publisher at books@daveburgessconsulting.com.

Published by Dave Burgess Consulting, Inc.
San Diego, CA
DaveBurgessConsulting.com

Library of Congress Control Number: 2021930069
Paperback ISBN: 978-1-951600-72-3
Ebook ISBN: 978-1-951600-73-0

Cover and interior design by Liz Schreiter
Editing and production by Reading List Editorial:
readinglisteditorial.com

Contents

Foreword by Merve Lapus 1

Introduction: My Why 4

    Digital Leadership Spotlight: Braeden Mannering 9

    Parent Vignette: Amber Coleman-Mortley. 12

CHAPTER 1: KIDS THESE DAYS   15

    How Are Kids Different Today? 18

    Our Human Needs 20

    Child and Adolescent Development: What to Expect and
When to Worry. 24

    Digital Leadership 29

    Try This! Strategies for Your Toolbox: Create Device-Free Times
and Zones. 30

    Try This! Create an Environment of Security and Curiosity. 35

    Parent Vignette: Genevieve V. Georget 37

    Digital Leadership Spotlight: Khloe Thompson. 39

CHAPTER 2: WHEN, WHERE, AND HOW MUCH?   41

    Let Kids' Interests Lead. 42

    Brick Wall, Jellyfish, and Backbone Parents 43

    When Should I Give My Child a Cell Phone? 46

    What Content and How Much Time Online Is Appropriate?. 48

    What Does Parental Involvement Actually Mean? 50

    How Can I Approach Restrictions? 51

    Try This! Strategies for Your Media Mentor Toolbox 55

    Digital Leadership Spotlight: Wizard and Wonder Chopra 60

    Parent Vignette: Valerie Lewis 63

CHAPTER 3: SOCIAL MEDIA   65

    What Is Social Media and What Are the Risks? 67

    The Dangers of Social Media 70

    Social Media and Mental Health 72

    What Should I Know about the Apps My Kids Want?. 74

    When Is the Right Time for Social Media? 84

    How Do I Protect My Child from Fake and Misleading News? 85

    Media Is a Construct 87

Media Has Special Interests. 88

Media Contains Value Messages. 89

Digital Leadership Spotlight: Anahit Hakobyan. 90

How Can I Help My Child Develop a Positive Online Presence?. . . . 91

How Can My Child Use Social Media for Their Future? 92

Try This! Strategies for Your Social Media Toolbox 94

Parent Vignette: Nicholas Clayton. 100

Digital Leadership Spotlight: Louie DaCosta 101

CHAPTER 4: GAMING   103

Are Video Games Really Bad for My Child? 104

How Much Time Is Appropriate and How Can I
Spot Addiction? 106

How Can I Keep My Child Safe Online?. 109

How Can Gaming Benefit My Child in the Future? 110

Try This! Strategies for Your Gaming Toolbox. 113

Parent Vignette: LIsa Monthie 117

CHAPTER 5: CYBERBULLYING   119

What Is the Relationship between Bullying
and Cyberbullying? 120

Subtweeting, Vaguebooking, Snitchtagging, Ghosting: What Does
Cyberbullying Look Like? 123

What Should I Do if My Child Is Cyberbullied?. 124

What Will Happen if My Child Stands Up to a Bully? 125

When to Worry. 126

Apps to Pay Attention To 127

Counteract Cyberbullying: The Science of Kindness 128

Try This! Strategies for Your Anti-Cyberbullying Toolbox 130

Digital Leadership Spotlight: Olivia Van Ledtje 137

Parent Vignette: Shelley Burgess. 138

CONCLUDING THOUGHTS: NOW WHAT?   141

Endnotes. 144

Acknowledgments. 152

About the Author. 153

More from Dave Burgess Consulting, Inc.. 155

Foreword
by Merve Lapus

Growing up in a new country as a young immigrant of color, I did not know the value of my voice. As a matter of fact, I felt the pressure to mute my words and my presence. I was sheltered from information, forced to follow a narrow line of expected behavior. "Don't call attention to yourself," I was told daily. The only space I had to amplify my voice was in an education system that valued processes and communication foreign to me. Opportunities for growth didn't necessarily run in my direction, so I had to do my own paving, often using third-rate materials and working ten times as hard to get half the distance.

Now, as a father of two amazing children and living at a time when information, access, and creativity are just a swipe and tap away, I have an opportunity to help my kids delineate their own limitations and help them on their paths. But the pace of life has increased since I was a child, and experiences that were often spread over days or weeks can now be wrapped up in scrolling on a device in literally just a couple of hours in a single day. Technology continues to grow in its ubiquity, and our kids are growing up in an era whey they—and the screens in front of them—have the potential to always be "on." They're bombarded with messages, and it's become far too easy for their voices to get drowned out. As a parent, I must both model how technology can be used effectively to effect positive change and provide my kids with a platform that amplifies their voices.

Today, ensuring that our children's voices are heard and developed is not only important, it's essential. Empowering them to assess how they are feeling, communicate their needs, and amplifying constructive change will help us to prepare young people for an ever-evolving future. Agency is an essential foundation to building leadership skills. As parents, educators, and community members, we all play a role in deciding whether the tech our children use is passive and consuming or active and engaging. We can redefine what it means to raise our kids to be leaders. We live in an age where we are not just teaching our kids to be the leaders of tomorrow but empowering them to be the leaders of today.

Much as we parents/caregivers have learned so much from our own networks—professional and personal—our kids are learning so much from theirs. Technology is no longer just a tool for learning, play, and community. Technology now operates as a space. One teen in a focus group said it well: "My parents just don't get it, I'm not addicted to social media, I'm addicted to my friends!" Social media has become a place for ongoing social engagement.

We know that our kids are going to use their platforms to connect and share, so it is important that we reinforce their foundation for empathy, ethics, morality, and integrity. We might never catch up to the tech know-how of our kids, but we can ensure that they are operating with the character and ideals we've passed along to them. Coupling our guidance and support with their curiosity and drive to connect is an essential part of developing them as leaders.

Youth voice can drive engagement! It is easy for anyone to make a lot of noise, but real power comes when our voices are truly heard. As an educator, take the time to learn from your students and empower them with the knowledge that they can own many parts of their learning. As a parent, know that kids are growing up with complex issues and experiences that require a supportive and helpful disposition, not punitive reactions. Our kids are going to need us by their sides as they explore their voices and take on issues that they are passionate about. They will make a load of mistakes, and they will look for guidance. That guidance could very easily come from someone in their network, but it will be much more powerful if it comes from you. How do you do all of this? I'll leave that to the next hundred or so pages to guide you.

I am excited that you are taking the time to dive into these important ideas with Jennifer Casa-Todd to explore how to raise digital leaders. I have learned a lot from Jennifer through the years, though, believe it or not, I have never once met her in person (just a webchat or two). She has been an extension of my learning network, and we have shared resources and guidance over platforms but never a cup of tea. This is the world our kids are growing up in. This is the world that we, as parents, hope that they will thrive within.

Jump in with an open mind, and be ready to redefine your curiosities and assumptions as Jennifer leads you through research, perspective, and even a little strategy. Tech will continue to evolve, and our kids will experiment, but we have an opportunity to help them harness their voices on more accessible megaphones. What will you do to make sure their voices are heard? How will you make sure they are represented? What can you do to journey alongside them to show what leadership is all about? How will you make sure that we are empowering our kids to use tech and not just letting tech use them? These are big questions, but if you aren't prepared to face them, how will you help your kids take the lead on all of their big ideas?

Introduction:
My Why

The idea for this book was planted in 2016 when a woman started to cry in the middle of my presentation at a technology conference. I was speaking to a room full of educators shortly before my first book, *Social LEADia: Moving Students from Digital Citizenship to Digital Leadership*, was officially published. I shared stories about students I had met who were using technology and social media to learn and to share learning, to empower others and to promote causes that were important to them, and to make a positive difference in the lives of others. I spoke about digital leadership, highlighting examples of students using technology to make a difference in the world, and I asserted that, contrary to popular belief, technology and social media aren't destroying the world. Then, from the corner of my eye, I noticed a woman at the back of the room crying—actually, almost sobbing. I was so perplexed. I remember wondering if I should stop my presentation to offer her a tissue. In the end, I asked if she was OK and joked that I had never had someone cry at one of my presentations before. Afterward, when I spoke to this woman, she shared that she had left her almost one-year-old with her mother-in-law in order to attend this conference and that, during my presentation, she had realized she was carrying an immense fear for the kind of world she had brought her child into; she was scared by the news headlines, and she felt ill-equipped to raise a child in a world that was so very different from the one in which she herself had been raised. Although I addressed a group of educators that day, her response was that of a mom. That encounter has stayed in my heart ever since.

Unfortunately, many parent presentations around the use of technology and social media are quite negative. I have been an audience member at a parent night where the speaker went on at length about the terrifying dangers of the online world. I recall looking at the other parents in the room, who seemed just as scared and uncomfortable as I was. Then I boldly asked a question: "Now what?" It was the speaker's turn to look uncomfortable. Some of the other parents looked grateful. One parent raised a tentative hand and added, "I came here hoping for ideas and strategies, and I am leaving with fear in my heart and nothing to help me." She was absolutely right. The fact is, technology and social media are part of our world. Our kids' future careers may be directly or indirectly correlated with the tech industry. Being critical and skeptical are important, but that's not going to help us to raise our kids. I realized very quickly that teachers aren't the only ones who need strategies and support to understand how to leverage technology and social media in positive ways; parents need it even more. Thus, I added a new presentation to my roster: Raising Digital Leaders. And I vowed to write this book.

I have been passionately reading, sharing, and writing about the topic of social media and its impact for many years. The more I research and the more I travel across Canada and the United States to talk with students, teachers, and parents, the more I recognize that many parents share an uncertainty around the whens, wheres, and hows of our fast-changing technology, along with a fear that it will invade and destroy our families.

What are your fears? Are they the same as mine? Are you fearful that your child will become a zombie, like those portrayed in the media? Are you afraid your child won't know how to communicate with others, how to hold actual conversations? Are you worried that your child will be the victim of an online predator or cyberbully? Are you concerned that one online mistake will forever ruin your child's life and future job prospects?

Or maybe, like some of the other parents I have met, you aren't necessarily fearful, but you worry about how much is too much. One parent admitted to me: "I love the iPad. My daughter is so quiet when I give it to her. I can get dinner made or take a shower. I have no idea if this is impacting my child's brain, but some days I am just so tired I don't care as much as I should." That, friends, is reality.

Add to this the fact that many of us saw our world and our use of technology irrevocably change because of the COVID-19 pandemic. If the tensions around technology use and screen time were high before, we suddenly had to add remote learning, social distancing, and a whole lot of unstructured time with nowhere to go to the equation.

Parenting today is hard, and when we give our kids tech, it is often with a sense of guilt mixed with relief. I had tons of fear, and lots of guilt, and still more fear when it came to my kids' technology use. My thinking only changed when my daughter Sydney was in tenth grade and applying for a summer job. Her interview was held over Skype, and we did our best beforehand to practice a few questions she might be asked. During the interview, I was crouched in the other room, craning my neck to listen to the questions, while trying to remain out of sight of the webcam. I was so proud of her answers. Then she was asked, "What social media are you on, and what will I learn about you if I go there?" We hadn't role-played that one. I'm not sure why because at the time I was a literacy consultant at the district level and was leading professional development around the use of technology. In that moment, I recognized that I had spent so much time as a parent telling my kids what *not* to do online that I hadn't really spent any time showing them what they *could* do. I spent a lot of time supporting their passions and encouraging them to be leaders, to stand up for themselves, and to be good people and students, but I always focused on what these things looked like in person, not online. When it came to their online interactions, I allowed the headlines to make me fearful and controlling.

Not long after, I met George Couros, author of *The Innovator's Mindset,* who would become a good friend and mentor to me. I really took to heart his definition of digital leadership as "using the vast reach of technology and social media to improve the lives, well-being, and circumstances of others." I had never thought to look at technology through that lens. More importantly, it never occurred to me to exercise that perspective when modeling the use of technology and social media for my own children. I was too paranoid about the potential risks.

What I soon came to understand, however, is that some parents out there are doing the opposite: they mentor their kids to be leaders in online spaces. I met kids who were leveraging technology so differently than I had ever imagined. They were making a difference on- and offline. The revelation I had meeting these kids led me to write my first book, *Social LEADia,* where I was able to share their awesome stories. It also led me to research the impact adult mentorship has on students using social media as part of my project for my master's degree in education.

Thus, I purposely talk about digital leadership and not just leadership. As a mom and educator, I want my kids to develop leadership skills. I want my kids to stand up for others, to teach others, to mentor and motivate others, to use their voices for good, to lead the way for others to be kind. Do I think my kids will become CEOs or run our country? Maybe. Maybe not. But it doesn't really matter. Regardless of what their career choices will be or where their life journey may take them, I can help my kids develop leadership skills that will serve them well in the future. Today, *digital* is a part of learning and working, and leadership in online spaces can open up opportunities for our children as they mature into adults.

Based on the findings of my research and the ongoing work I have done for a Google Innovator project, I have come to a definition of digital leadership: the ability to use technology, especially social media, to develop and model a positive digital identity. I use the LEAD acronym, which stands for learn, and share learning; empathy and perspective; aware; and digital role models.

Learn & Share Learning:
Digital Leaders see the value of technology and social media beyond entertainment

Empathy & Perspective:
Digital Leaders ensure that they consider tone, language, & multiple points of view when posting online.

Aware:
Digital Leaders understand how media works.

Digital Role Models:
Digital Leaders use technology and social media positively to make the world a better place.

@JCasaTodd, 2021

This book is organized around the LEAD framework, my own experiences as a mom and educator, the questions parents have asked me, research I have done that has helped me, and tools for you to try. In Digital Leadership Spotlights, I also showcase kids I have met who have been mentored by parents or another caring adult. I am not a psychologist or a behaviorist, and I am nowhere near a perfect parent. But, friends, there is no such thing as a perfect parent. When I talk to parents and teachers, when I share with them ideas and strategies, there is a noticeable shift. People leave my sessions saying, "I got this!" or "I thought I was the only one dealing with this!" After one of my parent talks, one parent said, "We need more opportunities to have these conversations and share strategies." This is why I have also included parent vignettes, which share the perspectives of other parents. It is important that we recognize that

BRAEDEN MANNERING

In 2013, at the age of nine, Braeden Mannering started an organization he named 3B: Brae's Brown Bags, which provides bags of healthy food and clean water to homeless and low-income populations in need. Each bag contains at least three healthy snacks, water, and a personal letter from Mannering that lists contact information for further assistance. In 2015, he launched the 3B Ripples program to expand the reach of the program beyond Delaware by setting up student chapters in communities across the country. Participating students receive education about hunger and poverty to promote understanding and empathy. Students then assemble bags of water, snacks, and service information to give to those in need. Mannering has provided more than 15,000 healthy bags, raised more than $72,000, and recruited 3,800 volunteers to help end hunger.

Since the beginning of 3B, Braeden has pitched his ideas and shared related content using Facebook, Twitter, YouTube, and Instagram. He also has a blog that is updated as needed with news and announcements. Between the social media platforms and blog, he is able to consistently reach over 7,800 people. These avenues have helped him network and partner with other agencies and youth groups who are changing the world.

there is no one way to do this parenting thing. We all benefit from listening and sharing with one another.

Whether your child is two or twenty-two, here's what I am hoping this book will do for you:

- Act as a conversation starter for you and the people in your parenting circles;
- Give you ideas and strategies for dealing with digital dilemmas in your family;
- Provide you with my perspective and those of other parents so you recognize you are not alone;
- Offer research that will help you know what is "normal" and when to worry;
- Show examples of kids being awesome on- and offline; and
- Present you with ideas for how to foster digital leadership in your own children.

Only rarely does this book offer specific advice connected to specific tools. Let's face it, when you pick up this book, the tools I am sharing might already be obsolete. Or maybe the tool I am writing about isn't the one your kids are using. Instead, I have laid out strategies you can add to your parenting toolbox that can be applied to a variety of situations. (I do have video tutorials in the chapter resources on my website, jcasatodd.com.)

I have carefully curated evidence-based strategies and resources that you can use to create the conditions for healthy technology habits and help your child build the skills and competencies they will need to succeed and lead today and in the future. I hope to provide balance to some of the fear-mongering out there, which, frankly, isn't very helpful. And it is my hope that this book will begin or continue conversations in your own family and community about how we support this next generation of leaders. I then invite you to bring those conversations and your ideas online to the private Facebook group I have created, Raising Digital Leaders, or the Instagram page @RasingDigitalLeaders.

Let's Talk about It

- What qualities would you wish your child to possess as they grow up both online and offline?
- What do you and your family value most?
- What are your biggest tech worries and struggles?

AMBER COLEMAN-MORTLEY

director of social engagement at iCivics, former teacher, mom

When online distance learning started due to shelter-in-place restrictions, I needed additional learning experiences because my daughters, Sofia, Garvey, and Naima, were finishing school-work rather quickly. And we all know that when boredom sets in with kids, a variety of unintended results emerge. I wanted to pursue something more creative to allow them opportunities to learn digital media skills while also providing space for them to have a voice on some of the most pressing matters at the moment. That's how the *Let's K12 Better* podcast came about. Right now we have a pretty decent sound setup thanks to their father and his expertise, but the first couple episodes were very bare-bones. I mean, we recorded them on my iPhone and pasted them together in GarageBand. I had to figure out hosting and sound editing (still learning). We worked together on the show outline and what elements we wanted to return to each week.

This has been a beautiful process, and though we are learning as we go, it's been wonderful to hear my daughters' thoughts and opinions about the world. None of what you'll hear on the podcast is me telling my kids what to do or say. Everything is from their vantage point, and it's all their ideas. Obviously we have a pre-podcast conversation before recording, just so I know what follow-up questions to ask or what kind of mindset that they're in before we start recording. But, essentially, it's just their ideas. I believe that children, particularly younger children, and particularly children of color, need to have a space to work on concepts like:

- *What do I believe in?*
- *What are the things that I know to be true?*
- *How can I challenge myself and then move into conversations with others?*
- *How do I challenge other people and help my peers to think critically about an issue?*
- *How do we collaborate on ideas together?*

Through the *Let's K12 Better* podcast, the kids are learning how to answer these broader questions. Even if no one listens, we are still holding these family conversations, and I'm still challenging them to think critically and build their own voices. That was the impetus for starting this project and the overarching goal for this podcast—learning how to use your voice.

As a person who has done her fair share of social media marketing, I'm always talking to my kids about building brands and how "brand building" in this age is super important. When people search for your name, what should come up? What do you want to be associated with who you are? With this, my children are really building their own brand. They're controlling the narrative about who they are.

Lots of parents are leery of technology use by kids. Technology is a tool, just like fire, an ax, a fishing rod, a pencil, or any other device we use to make life more convenient. But we can't just give our kids these tools and walk away; we have to teach our children how to use them. My middle schooler has a smartphone, and so do her friends. She realizes that kids are being exposed to content that is questionable and sometimes racist. We cannot equate close proximity with safety when our kids are in this virtual world. Just because they might be sitting next to you in the car or on the sofa doesn't mean they're not at risk. Kids need the skills to navigate digital spaces. They need to be able to not only address cyberbullying but also race-based cyberbullying, sexting, talking to strangers in chat rooms, or even basics like how to search and separate helpful from harmful information using media literacy.

Our family is pretty close already, which is wonderful. We have established chemistry that allows us to have these rich and meaningful discussions on the podcast and offline. This is primarily because these conversations have been going on since my kids were old enough to say words and express opinions in short sentences. When they were as young as two years old and even younger, I've asked them in a variety of ways: *"How do you feel about your world?"* This has conditioned them to understand that they have a voice, that I respect their opinions, that they can trust me with their thoughts and dreams. We have a dialogue centered on the trust that when they say something to me, they know that I'm listening.

1

Kids These Days

My daughter Sydney was born in 2000. When I was pregnant with her, the news headlines every single day were about the end of the world. With Y2K looming, I was terrified that I would not live to meet my baby girl. I literally cried myself to sleep some nights, and on New Year's Eve 1999, I suffered through the most terrifying nightmares. What would I wake up to in the morning? I suspect this feeling of doom is familiar to many parents as they are bombarded by news headlines that tell us how social media is destroying the world. Even though my kids are very respectful both on- and offline, there were (and are) many days when I looked at my kids on their devices and feared they would become everything I was reading about. As I have fielded questions from parents, interacted with my own students, and mentored students in a global student-led chat, I have come to realize that I am not the only one with fears. But fear doesn't help us. We need to use the wisdom of the past, be mindful of the present reality, and look toward a bright and hopeful future for our kids. We can long all we want for the days of old, when our parents let us out in the morning and called us back at suppertime, when we didn't have smartphones or social media, but that world doesn't exist anymore. We can also wish for a society where your online footprint doesn't matter, but the fact is, 85 percent of employers say positive online content influences hiring decisions. We live in a world filled with opportunities and challenges that have never existed before.

As a mom and educator, I have seen the gradual change from little to no technology in our home to being fully connected. First, my husband and I had to come to terms with rules around using the DS, a popular gaming console launched in the early 2000s. We then moved to iPod Touches, with the beginnings of messaging and all of the problems that came with this new way of communicating, and finally to smartphones and hormones. YouTube only became a thing in 2005, when my oldest child was five and my youngest was two. Yet many of today's children (and perhaps even you) have only known a world of smartphones, Netflix, YouTube, and Siri—a world where you can order something on Amazon and it arrives the same day. If there was one thing that became very evident as a result of the global pandemic, it is how much technology has advanced and how useful it is. If COVID-19 had happened ten years ago, the experience would have been very different. In 2020, we were able to stay connected to loved ones, continue to work, shop, and even bank. I have to continue to remind myself that, for the majority of us parenting right now, our children were born in a different century than us—a different millennium even! Even knowing the benefits of technology, we continue to get overwhelmed by fear and uncertainty.

"Get off your phone! What is so important that you need to be on it right now?" As these words came out of my mouth, I realized I was scolding my daughter exactly the same way my own mother had scolded me. The only difference was that I hadn't been on a smartphone, I had been in my family room on the family's rotary phone, the long phone cord pulled as far as I could stretch it so I could distance myself from the rest of the family seated in front of the television. (Now there are very few kids who have ever even seen a rotary phone with a cord and maybe you yourself have never owned one!) I remember learning how to speak in pig latin so my family wouldn't know what I was saying. And I remember that, if I could have, I would have spent all day on that phone. Of course, in those days, if I was on the phone, no one else could be, since we only had one family line. It didn't take me long to memorize our family's phone patterns: my nonna would call at a certain time, then my aunt. I would quietly get on the phone in the in-between times to maximize the time I could talk to my friends. I could never have imagined a time when you could be in a group chat with several friends simultaneously to check what your friends were wearing or to tell them about your latest encounter with that cute guy in your math class. I often challenge the idea that kids are addicted to their phones; they are actually addicted to talking to their friends (we will address addiction later).

When we worry about "kids these days," we forget aspects of our own adolescent development. We remember nostalgically the time spent playing outside, but we live in a different world. Not many parents I have talked to would send their child outside for eight hours without any contact with home, and some kids simply don't live in communities where outside play spaces are even available. When I was a kid, we flailed around in the back of our car without a thought about seat belts. I ate cookies and coffee for breakfast every day when I was in elementary school. Yup, you heard it, no organic granola or steel-cut oats with superfood toppings for me. (When my kids found this out, I gave in to sugary cereals on weekends.) I'm not saying I was raised badly or that we have gone too far today. I am simply stating it is different, and we need to take a look back from time to time and think about what we were really like as kids.

Obviously, the world into which our kids have been born is vastly different. We live in a world where we can 3-D print a human heart, where our fridge can create shopping lists for us, and where cars can drive themselves. We live in a world where we have access to information about all of the tragedies and crime happening around the globe and where it seems like suicide, depression, and anxiety have run rampant. And in our world, social media is seemingly to blame for so much of what is happening. Although we will talk more about some of the research I've done around these topics, I first want to address a big question.

How Are Kids Different Today?

When I am invited to speak to groups of parents, I always show a short clip:

> Opening scene: Pregnant woman screaming in a hospital bed. She is red-faced, sweating, and in obvious pain. Her husband is clutching her hand.

> Next frames: Her baby is born, cuts his own umbilical cord (after consulting Google on how to do it), and then proceeds to take a selfie with the doctor, dress himself, and crawl right out of the hospital. All the adults watch in semi-horror and semi-awe.

> Final frame: Born for the Internet (company logo).

It's this kind of thinking that gets us into trouble. The world has changed in so many ways, but, despite the smartphones and devices, kids are inherently the same. We are made up of the same DNA we always have been. Remember that parent who talked about her iPad as a magical device that allowed her to get dinner made or take a shower? When my kids were little, we didn't have iPads, but it was still technology that I put in front of them. In my case, it was the magical Teletubbies. Every time I put on that show so I could get dinner made or just sit and relax for a few minutes, I felt an incredible sense of guilt. It was like my kids became zombies—quiet little zombies. Is that normal? Um, yes. Did I let my kids watch for ten hours a day until their brains grew into mush? Of course not! Let's agree right now that guilt (although a natural by-product of parenting) has no business here. You picked up this book because you want to learn more about tech and leadership and how all of it will impact your kids, so let's throw guilt to the curb.

You need to know that technology has always caused panic, fear, and anxiety in people. I grew up in an age where we heard every day about how television was going to rot our brains and how music videos were going to be the death of society as we knew it. Think about this quote, attributed to Plato speaking to Socrates in ancient Greece thousands of years ago:

> The children now love luxury; they have bad manners, contempt for authority; they show disrespect for elders and love chatter in place of exercise. Children are now tyrants, not the servants of their households. They no longer rise when elders enter the room. They contradict their parents, chatter before company, gobble up dainties at the table, cross their legs, and tyrannize their teachers.[1]

Even thousands of years ago, adults were complaining about kids. I try to remember this every time I turn on the news, read the paper, or hear someone say, "Kids these days." When I see a headline that claims technology and social media are destroying the world, I usually read the entire article or research paper, and almost always, there is a paragraph near the end that acknowledges the many other factors that contribute to the problem at hand (e.g., narcissism, suicide, violence). Things are always more complicated than the headlines suggest. A study about online risk showed that "teenagers' explorations in the digital world are not very different from those by earlier generations; the platform differs, not the behaviors. Teens use digital and mobile technologies for many purposes, risk is not always negative, and opportunities to fail safely can be valuable too."[2]

The mantra I repeat to myself when I am in a panic is this: Every generation has complained about its youth, and every generation has been afraid of technological advances.

When the printing press came along, some feared that access to the written word was a terrible idea. Today, literally anyone can publish their ideas for all the world to see (in fact, a few of the students I feature in this book are authors and still in high school). This is amazing, isn't it? We can't let fear overtake our wonder. We need to find a way to make technology work for us, not the other way around.

Breathe in.

Breathe out.

Our Human Needs

Have you ever seen a diagram illustrating Maslow's hierarchy of needs? Maslow was a psychologist whose theory continues to drive the way we look at what kids need to grow to their full potential. It's a theory that helps me to understand my kids (and even myself) better.

In some iterations floating around the internet, Wi-Fi is added to the bottom tier as a basic need (clearly a joke—or is it?). Maslow suggests that kids need to get their basic needs—food, water, warmth, and rest—met, feel safe and secure, and have a sense of belonging before they can become their best selves. Although there is some disagreement about the hierarchy itself and the extent to which his ideas originated from the Blackfoot Nation, I find it useful to think about the research around Maslow's framework in relation to the use of electronic devices.

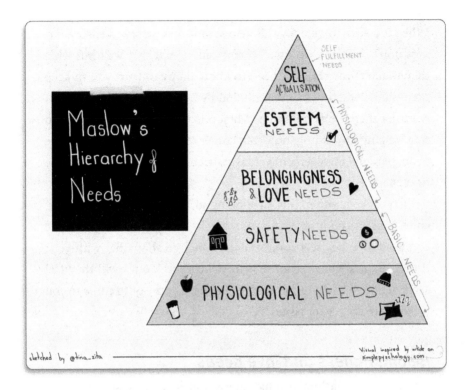

Physiological needs

Physiological needs are our human needs for food and rest. Of all the research I have read, the biggest concern with early and frequent use of devices is that growing brains need sleep. As a result, devices in bedrooms are not a thing in my house—not for our kids and not for us as parents. More on that later.

Safety and security

Safety and security, according to Maslow's hierarchy, are a must. A regular routine is also connected to safety and security. That night-time routine of brushing your teeth, reading a book, a kiss goodnight, and lights out can be magical. Although the same routine isn't always possible, the more a child can anticipate what is going to happen and predict transitions, the greater the likelihood they will feel secure.

When it comes to devices, this also means that we try to ensure our kids don't meet the wrong strangers online and that we limit what they watch. Your children need to know they can trust you to keep them safe. Sometimes I say it out loud when my kids wonder why I won't let them do something: "My job is to love you and keep you safe." (Being unyielding, however, comes at a cost. We will talk more about parental involvement versus restriction and surveillance in the next chapter.)

Consider another way of looking at safety and security. Your child happens upon an inappropriate site. They feel scared, maybe confused. Do they feel comfortable enough to share that with you? If they do, and your response is to yell (or freak out), will they feel secure enough to share something like that again—or to come to you when there are bigger issues?

Belongingness and love needs

According to Maslow, belongingness and love are essential needs that lead to you becoming the best person you can be. If kids are not feeling loved or valued, they will crave this validation and go elsewhere to get it. So many of the issues we see with provocative selfies or at-risk behavior stem from a lack of self-esteem, belonging, or self-worth. There are many, many factors that contribute to this, and you as a parent or guardian cannot take responsibility for all of them. You need to know, however, that a child who struggles with belonging or feeling loved may be more likely to engage in risky behaviors. This is not anyone's fault, nor is it a reason to feel guilty. It just is.

That means we need to be particularly mindful to make kids feel extra loved. I try to remind myself that if my kids don't feel like they belong, they will do whatever it takes to find someone who will make them feel that they do. Belonging and self-worth start with validation and attention. It is natural for adolescents to seek peer approval, but well before they are teens, they need to develop a healthy sense of themselves, which will help them make it through what my husband and I affectionately called "the horror years" (thankfully, both my girls have made it back to being reasonable and pleasant humans again).

Esteem needs

Henry Jenkins, a media scholar and professor at the University of Southern California, has really helped me to think about ways to validate our children when it comes to their online world. He says that kids need their parents to recognize that what they are doing online can be valuable, in the same way we would go to their concerts or recitals and listen to them play an instrument (perhaps not so well). Are we telling them that they are wasting their time, or are we helping them to see a path toward a future where they can use the skills they are gaining?[3]

We will talk more about video games in a later chapter, but think about how the repetition of the same levels in a game can contribute to a sense of certainty and security, how in the game a child can feel a sense of accomplishment and prestige, and how their need for belonging can be met when they connect with others in an online gaming community. If the only time you felt truly worthwhile or valuable was when you were gaming, would you want to do anything else?

Connection

In rethinking Maslow's hierarchy, people have argued that, while the needs make sense, placing them into the form of a triangle, with one need requiring fulfillment before another can be addressed, doesn't. For example, there are kids living in terrible poverty who are happy and feel like they belong. At the center of this newer thinking on Maslow's theory is the idea of connection: that in fact, our fundamental needs stem from a connectedness to all the other needs and to other people. We saw this during COVID-19 when our inability to connect with others caused feelings of loss, overwhelm, and anxiety in many people. Another subtle change in the rethinking of Maslow's hierarchy of needs is the connection between esteem and reputation (both on- and offline), which we will talk about when we discuss digital identity.

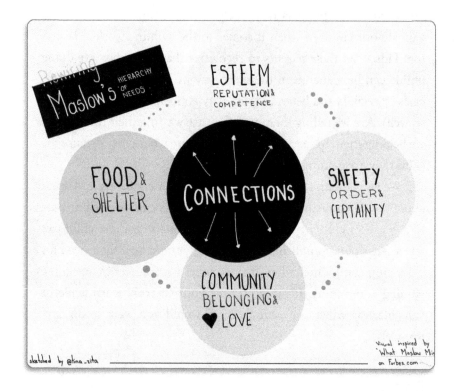

Child and Adolescent Development: What to Expect and When to Worry

What I find really relieves some of the anxiety around technology use is to understand what behavior is and is not typical when it comes to development. Please remember, I am not a psychologist, so it may be worth seeking additional information and help if your situation falls under the "when to worry" markers I set out in this book.

Think back for a moment to when your baby was born. You'll likely recall the list of baby milestones your doctor gave you or you read in a book. You might also remember how easy it was to become somewhat obsessed with when your child reached those milestones compared to others in your baby group. Though sometimes being aware of those baby milestones made us feel less nervous about how our children were developing, sometimes the opposite was true, and they made us a little more stressed out.

I'm sure you can imagine how nervous we were when every other child in our playgroup was running around at thirteen months, while our little Sydney was happy to sit and read a book or complete a puzzle and rarely even pulled herself up at all. Of course, she did eventually walk, and then run, and at some later point, we stopped seeing those milestone checklists (or maybe stopped being so preoccupied by them). But still, we often wondered, like when our kids were having an all-out temper tantrum in the grocery store, "This can't be normal, can it?" We had heard about the terrible twos, but my mother-in-law, a kindergarten teacher for most of her adult life, told us to watch out for the "f*#ing fours." Truly. I don't, however, remember comparing my nine- or twelve- or fifteen-year-old's development to that of other kids or using any kind of checklist. Having said that, there were many days when I wondered if my kids were grumpier or happier or messier or more or less attentive than most kids their age, and what fascinated me was that when I did get together with other parents and compare notes, many of them were experiencing the same things. (Trust me friend, the BEST thing I ever did was be totally vulnerable and real with a few of my trusted friends, asking them: "I am really struggling with something. What strategies do you use with your kids?") While I am not a neuroscientist or a psychologist, having an overall sense of how children and adolescents develop has really helped me to parent and teach.

Childhood development

The Centers for Disease Control and Prevention (CDC) offers good guidelines for parents and divides childhood development into social/emotional, physical, and cognitive development up to the age of five (there's even an app). The CDC tells us that kids up to the age of five need to interact with the physical world. They need to touch and build and figure out and turn the pages of books. Because kids absorb and observe everything, parental modeling is important for almost everything (e.g., eating, exercising, safety). The CDC recommends that we offer simple choices to children ages three to five as their brains are making connections and lots of learning is happening.

As children get older, their brains continue to grow and develop along with their bodies. The CDC recommends that we continue to encourage children ages six to nine to solve problems with our support and that we recognize that peer relationships and independence become growing concerns. Attention spans begin to increase, and the capacity for learning about others also increases.

Adolescent development

As kids move into early adolescence, they are concerned with emotional rewards, are sensitive to social reputation, and are maturing in terms of higher-order thinking skills. Basically, the brain is growing and working to make connections to solve problems and negotiate ties to parents and friends. So, one minute, adolescents will curl up for a hug and a story, and the next minute they'll want nothing to do with you!

Most of my experience lies in adolescent development (ages twelve to eighteen). When I was the literacy consultant for my district, the Ministry of Education published a guide for teachers that was anchored to how adolescents develop and learn. I found it very useful in my professional role, but I found it even more useful as a mom. Whenever I thought my kids were the worst kids on the planet, this guide helped me realize they were actually completely normal in terms of adolescent development. My experiences as a teacher also helped me to realize the extent to which teens develop in radically varying degrees.

One day, I was supervising the weight room when a group of ninth-grade boys was using it. One of them was slender and short, while another towered over the rest. Some of the boys clearly felt comfortable in their new bodies, while others seemed to be tripping over themselves. A similar comparison could be made among the girls: some of them looked like women when they entered high school and others like little girls.

In terms of physical development, adolescents are

- typically engaged in less physical activity;
- experiencing increases in strength, energy levels, stamina, and sexual maturation at different times and rates;
- feeling fatigued at various times during the day (though this also sounds like me most days!);
- experiencing increased appetite and shifts in their eating habits; and
- experiencing a change in their sense of body image.

If we unpack this, we'll see that the lazy teenager who is changing their clothes a million times a day and who would rather sit on the couch than engage may make us absolutely crazy but is more typical than not. One of the recommendations for teaching adolescents based on these changes is to give them opportunities to move in class, to engage them in a critical analysis of media portrayals of the "perfect" male or female, and to create safe spaces for social and emotional learning.

Cognitively, adolescents are going through a period of brain growth. In fact, it has been hypothesized that the brain doesn't fully develop until a person is in their mid-twenties. During adolescence, typical cognitive behavior includes

- an increased ability to process and make connections;
- a desire to explore creative expression in a supportive environment;
- questioning and curiosity;
- concern with the present rather than planning for the future or thinking thoroughly about consequences; and
- development of the ability to focus on an idea or task by filtering irrelevant information.

As much as you may be unhappy with your teenager who is a disorganized mess, doesn't know what they want to do with their life, takes unnecessary risks, and questions authority, now you know that this is completely normal too.

Technology and the developing brain

So what happens when you take a child or adolescent who is developing normally neurologically and you bring them into a world where information is no longer consumed on a black-and-white page but a screen in which media potentially comes alive in front of them (augmented reality) or into which they themselves can become immersed in a game or a place (virtual reality); a world where they can literally ask a question out loud and get an answer (Google, Alexa, Siri); and where they can consume media whenever they want for as long as they want (TikTok, Netflix, YouTube, Hulu, Prime). Well, according to neuroscientist and author Dr. David Eagleman, having so much access to information does impact the adolescent brain, but he isn't convinced this necessarily means in a bad way. He shares that learning happens when you are curious about the answer, so it's not necessarily a bad thing to be able to ask Google something. Eagleman argues that our brains register signals, assign patterns and meaning to all of the signals they get, and figure out what to do with these patterns and meanings. Eagleman says that there isn't a lot to worry about because our brains are capable of so much and that, essentially, kids "can absorb a much bigger world than we were capable of when we grew up."[4]

I know my fear of information overload stems from my own failures at remembering things. Professor Michael Saling, neuropsychologist from the University of Melbourne and Austin Health, addresses this: "I get at least one patient a week who is convinced that forgetting things like car keys or picking up children is the result of a serious brain condition or early Alzheimer's. The truth is the expansion of the information age has happened so fast, it's bringing us face to face with our brains' limitations. Just because our computer devices have perfect memories, we think we should too."[5] I saw a meme once that made me literally laugh out loud. It said, "Some days, I astound myself with how brilliant I am and other days I leave my keys in the fridge." Totally me!

Saling reminds us that forgetfulness is a normal phenomenon that occurs when we push information out as new information comes in. When our brain gets overloaded, we become forgetful. Having said that, a lot of research suggests that our brains are not good at multitasking, even though we think they are, and giving our undivided attention and concentration to a single task is really important.[6]

Digital Leadership

When I think of kids these days, it is with a completely different lens: I know kids to be awesome. My book *Social LEADia* highlights kids who are digital leaders. They are leveraging social media and technology to learn and share learning, to empower others and support important causes, and to make a positive difference in the lives of others. I don't remember being as empathetic as many of my students are today, and I certainly didn't hear of kid entrepreneurs or authors when I was young. The kids I follow on social media have founded nonprofit organizations before they even started college or university! You will meet a few of these inspiring kids in this book.

One group of kids I studied for my master's degree in curriculum and technology was engaged in an Ontario Educational student chat (now Global Educational Student Chat). As I went through thousands of tweets and hours of YouTube videos, I discovered that, with adult (and peer) mentorship, these students were true LEADers online. They didn't necessarily have hundreds or thousands of followers, instead they used Twitter to act as role models for others (D). They were aware of a public audience and used that awareness to inspire others or to share causes they care about (A). Most importantly, these students modeled respectful behavior online for others and used Twitter to connect with other students in the world for the purpose of learning (L). One student shared how powerful it was to be able to learn from other students outside of her school and even community. It allowed her to understand others' perspectives (E). Because it is true that "you can't be what you can't see," it is important to expose our children to role models who use technology and social media to help make the world a better place. When we say "kids these days" in a derogatory way, we fail to see that kids have opportunities to make a difference at any age, if they are given the guidance they need. This doesn't mean we force our kids into leadership. Rather we should consider their passions and talents and help them flourish in person and online.

Try This! Strategies for Your Toolbox: Create Device-Free Times and Zones

The bedroom

When a device is in your room, the glow of the light or the notifications can interfere with REM sleep (the kind your body needs to restart). Many researchers and psychologists recommend that devices should not be in bedrooms. When I realized this recommendation was connected to a basic need (see Maslow's hierarchy) and when I read about the countless studies that connected lack of sleep to so many other problems, I decided this was one battle I was going to fight.

Starting when my kids were quite young, we decided that bedrooms and, more generally, the upstairs in our house were device-free zones. This became the norm, and I never had to worry about my kids not getting enough rest. However, in recent years, they have shared that they are the only ones who have this rule, and they will often ask for sleepovers at friends' houses so they can break it. They have argued that they need their phones as alarms, that they need music to sleep, and so on. My response to them: "How can we solve that problem and still make sure we don't have a device in our room that is not healthy for our brains at night?" Kids can be reasonable or unreasonable, but as parents, it's our job, whenever we know better, to do better. My husband and I have explained the why, and we have been careful to model this, which means that my husband and I do not bring devices into our bedroom. Beyond concerns about sleep, whenever parents have shared a story with me about a negative situation related to device use, it almost always seems to happen in the middle of the night and in the solitude of kids' rooms.

Every morning when we were young, my parents expected my sisters and me to make our beds. We were actually not even allowed to come downstairs until we were fully dressed and had made our beds. When I wanted to know why this was so important, the answer was, "Because you live under my roof, and you live by my rules." My parents hated a messy house. When I got married and moved away, the first thing I did when I woke up after my honeymoon was go downstairs without the bed made and in my pajamas! It was such a guilty pleasure.

When my kids were young, I never insisted they make their beds unless someone slept over because I hated my parents' rule and thought it was pointless. (My sister, on the other hand, cannot leave her room without making her bed and insists her own daughter make her bed.) For me, I didn't understand the why. If my parents had explained it by saying something like, "Our brains sometimes need order," or "A tidy room is something I really value when everything else is so unpredictable," I maybe would have insisted on it too. At this point, it would be really difficult to insist that my kids make their beds—not impossible, just really difficult. Bottom line, it is much easier to begin a routine when your kids are young, and a routine will be much more effective if your kids understand that your reasoning is connected to their health and well-being. Now that my daughter Sydney is in university, I can't regulate whether or not she keeps her device in her room, but I can feel better knowing I tried to instill good habits that she will bring to her own children if she chooses to have them. Isn't that all we can hope when it comes to raising our kids?

The car

Another good place to create a device-free zone is the car. Not only is this a best practice for safety's sake (distracted driving is a real problem), the reality is that the best conversations with your kids can happen when you are in the car together. This is because you aren't looking them in the eye, so their brain doesn't feel like it's being interrogated. There's also a lot of goofiness, music appreciation (maybe even singing as your kids roll their eyes), game playing, and gazing out the window that can happen as a result.

The dinner table

The dinner table is also mostly a device-free zone in my house. My family has been fortunate to be able to eat dinner together at least a couple of times a week, which allows us to connect with each other. When our kids were in elementary and middle school, we shared our favorite and least favorite parts of the day. For us, this was better than asking "How was your day?" and "What is one new thing you learned today?" because the answers were always "Fine" and "Nothing." This still worked when they were in high school, but I would often ask "Any new drama?" instead, as that seemed to elicit more conversation. Dinner conversations help kids understand your point of view and give them an opportunity to share stories. I find that dinner conversation also gives me insight into my kids' social lives, as well as what they find amusing and annoying.

So, why did I say "mostly device-free"? I found that the more in-depth our conversations became, the more we wanted to check something online to validate what one of us was saying. We have had heated discussions that required one of us to look up an answer we all disagreed upon—like which actor was in that movie we watched a million years ago. When we have extended family get-togethers, our devices come to the table so we can share photos or play an app created by Ellen DeGeneres called Heads Up. Frank Vetere, associate professor and director of the Microsoft Research Centre for Social Natural User Interfaces at the University of Melbourne, who researches human–computer interactions, challenges us to

> Consider a contemporary scenario where parents are telling their children not to bring their mobile phone to the dinner table because we prefer to talk to each other. What if we rethink that scenario and encouraged people to bring their devices to the dinner table in a way that motivates social rapport, well-being and family harmony?[7]

Now, I realize that not everyone has the opportunity to eat together, that families look different, and for some cultures, eating at the same time is not a valued custom. A few studies, however, have linked family mealtime with emotional well-being later in life. One Quebec study found family meals have long-term influences on children's biopsychosocial well-being.[8] A Hong Kong study linked family meals and family meal preparation to family health, happiness, and harmony and to mental and physical quality of life. This particular study determined that it was more about quality rather than quantity of family communication that promoted well-being.[9] The research supports that eating together and having family discussions even a couple of times a week with even only one parent present proves beneficial.

If you aren't sure what to talk about, the internet can help with this too. Southlake Baptist Church in Southlake, Texas,[10] shared fifty-two dinner discussion topics, including the following:

- When you are a parent, what do you think is going to be your most important rule you are going to have and have to enforce?
- If you could plan a dinner for our family at any location in the world, where would you plan it and why?
- If our family had our own cooking show on TV, what would be our specialties and style of food?

Dr. Kristen Mattson, posted a tweet about generating "Would you rather . . . ?" prompts for students to think about digital citizenship. When I saw her tweet, it made me think about what a great conversation starter that would be for our family. And so, I began to ask "would you rather" questions. "Would you rather have one good friend or a thousand Snapchat friends?" "Would you rather people think you are smart or pretty?" And don't just ask the questions; create a family rotation. The questions your child poses also reveal so much about their feelings and experiences.

Try This! Create an Environment of Security and Curiosity

I wonder . . .

Neuroscientist David Eagleman says that the best time for a child to learn is when they are curious. The "I wonder . . ." phrase can be powerful and magical. You see, when we pointedly ask about a topic, our tone may set off the fight-or-flight response in our brains: "Is my mom upset with me? Am I in trouble?" Consider the difference between saying "Get off that phone! Your brain is going to turn to mush!" and saying "I wonder why I feel so grumpy when I have been on my phone (or computer) for a long time."

In both scenarios, you are acknowledging that an excessive use of technology can affect moods, but the second brings in your own experience and also invites a conversation.

- I wonder if all families have the same rules about games we do.
- I wonder if this person is having a bad day because what they just said (or posted) was not very nice/appropriate.

We will see examples of "I wonder" statements in many chapters in this book.

Watch your tone

Keeping your tone calm is important. If your child's brain senses danger from your tone, a series of physical and emotional responses can be set off (usually in my house this involves yelling, storming off, and doors slamming). We need to reserve loud volumes and intense tones for dangerous situations.

Think aloud

This is another strategy you will see throughout the book because it is so powerful. This is about using your voice to share what you are thinking so your child has access to those thoughts and can learn from them in a nonthreatening way. I recommend using think-alouds way before your child is old enough for a device. Here are some ways you can model your thinking for your kids:

- **Attention:** "Wait. I am going to put my phone down to give you my full attention."
- **Multitasking:** "Research says humans are not good at multitasking. I am going to put my phone on its charger so I can focus on finishing this."
- **Bedtime:** "I am going to plug in my phone now and go up to bed because my brain needs to recharge."
- **Dinner table:** "I am going to put my phone on the charger so we can have an uninterrupted family conversation while we eat."
- **Kids these days:** "I saw the best news article about a young person who did something that could never have happened when I was young."
- **Belonging and esteem:** "I am just thinking about how much I love you." Or "I am really proud of how carefully you worked on that."

Breathe

Yup, I just wrote that into your toolkit. Sometimes what puts us into a complete panic is not as bad as we first think and can provide a good learning opportunity. When we panic, we may yell or scream and activate our kids' fight-or-flight instinct. Taking a deep breath and saying, "I am way too upset right now to deal with this" is a good strategy for a couple of reasons. First, it models the way you want your kids to approach something that is upsetting, and second, it gives you time to look at the situation practically to decide what the best course of action should be. Messed up? No guilt here.

GENEVIEVE V. GEORGET

mom, published writer, and storytelling editor in Ottawa, Ontario, Canada

I was at a wedding a while ago, sitting next to a grandmother who complained that kids who use digital devices aren't learning real values from their parents or learning anything of meaning at all.

I asked her, "Did your daughter have access to those things when she was growing up?"

"No, of course not," she answered.

"Because you didn't let her or because they didn't exist?"

"They didn't exist. Why?"

"Because it leads me to wonder how useful it is to sit here and judge another's parenting to a group of strangers when you could, instead, find ways to support that parent while they face challenges that didn't exist when you were raising your own children."

For the record, she didn't appreciate this feedback too much, and the conversation ended there. Having said that, I—along with a large number of my friends and family—don't appreciate getting told every single day that we're raising serial killers because we let our children use a paint-by-numbers app on our computers.

We are the first generation of parents having to raise children in this new world, and we're having to do so without much of a support system in place to help us navigate it. Truth be told, it's really hard and scary to be a parent right now. I can go online on any given day and stumble across fifteen articles dictating all the ways that I'm not parenting correctly, and I can do it all before nine in the morning. Granted, this is all I know as a parent and I have nothing to compare it to, but I can still boldly state that I would rather have your help than your criticism.

Are there immense challenges that come with this digital age? Absolutely. Are there huge imbalances that will have to be leveled out through the generations to come? No doubt about it. But every generation has had its struggles, and no generation has been perfect at managing them.

The truth is that this technology isn't going anywhere. The world isn't going to stop progressing because we don't like seeing kids with computers in their pockets. And it's not actually serving anyone (especially our children) to create a narrative around how terrible their future is as a result. That same technology allows my kids to Skype with their family who live in another country. It enables me to work from home so I can be more present with my family when they need me. And it brings the world's greatest minds and resources to our fingertips. We're all growing and learning and blindly trying to make our way.

So, here is my hope for us as parents: The next time we feel the urge to disparage our children's world because it doesn't look the same as our own, perhaps we can pause, breathe, and redirect ourselves. Perhaps, instead, we can turn to our friends, our children, our fellow parents, and ask, "How can I better support you as we navigate a world—and a future—that is different for all of us?"

Then we can hop on YouTube together and enjoy the greatest gift technology has ever given us: a never-ending stream of hilarious cat videos![11]

KHLOE THOMPSON

When Khloe Thompson was eight years old, she noticed an issue with homelessness in her community. Seeing women living on the street made Khloe feel sad, and she wanted to do something to help.

In 2015, Khloe started the Khloe Kares Foundation, a charity that caters to the homeless, does community service, and strives to provide a positive example. Since then, she has been able to help many women on the streets by giving out more than two thousand sturdy handmade Kare Bags that contain necessities like toothbrushes, toothpaste, soap, lotion, feminine hygiene products, and washcloths. Children, adults, and businesses often contribute by donating items and helping to pass out the Kare Bags around Los Angeles's Skid Row in Khloe's home state of California.

Khloe dedicates herself to serving others and giving back to her community. She enjoys visiting elementary schools and other youth-focused organizations like WE Day California and Born This Way Foundation, with the goal of inspiring other young people to find ways to make a difference in their community. Khloe has been invited to participate in community action programs across the country and has shared her story on television programs, in books and magazines, and on social media that has been viewed around the world, including publications and platforms like POPSUGAR, Huffington Post, and YouTube. Khloe has a heart of gold and has been blessed by God to have the gift of compassion for others. She is a true example of her belief that "no matter how old you are, you can make a difference!" Her leadership extends to her Instagram and Twitter accounts, where you can see Khloe's good deeds and positive example.

When, Where, and How Much?

Parenting has changed, and that can be truly frustrating and scary at times. Not only am I not a stay-at-home mom like my mom was but I also feel like so much of my job is tied to my email. My kids have actually said to me, "Mom, please put your phone down and listen to me when I tell you this." We are all trying our best, and believe me when I tell you that any person who looks like the perfect parent on Instagram (we will talk about that in the next chapter) is showing you a filtered version of their life. Even if you are rich enough to afford help, this parenting thing is confusing and hard. This chapter is built around the most commonly asked questions I get. If your burning question isn't one I tackle here, be sure to visit the Social LEADia: Raising (Digital) Leaders Facebook page, send me an email, or tag me @RaisingDigitalLeaders on Instagram to start a conversation about it.

Let Kids' Interests Lead

Fostering digital leadership in your kids is about recognizing when their interests are driving the time they spend online. I remember my friend Janice complaining about how much time her daughter spent editing films and playing with filters. Later her daughter went to film school and is now employed in the film industry. Our rules about screen time need to be balanced with our kids' passions. We must also consider how powerful it is for our kids to follow other student digital leaders, kids who are learning and sharing learning, empowering others without a voice, or making a positive difference. When I was writing *Social LEADia*, I met Aidan and Keeley Aird. Their parents gave them a fossil for special occasions, and both Keeley and Aidan grew to love science. They competed in science fairs and attended community events around their passion for science. Aidan soon realized that no one knew about all of the amazing scientists he was meeting, so he created a website called Developing Innovations where he highlighted them. He also created a Twitter account that he used to follow organizations and science-related content. His sister took his lead and began doing the same. Together, they created STEM Kids Rock, which they turned into a nonprofit organization. With STEM Kids Rock, Keeley and Aidan go into the community with all of their fossils and try to instill a passion for all things science. The time they spend online feeds their passion and interest in science but also led them to make connections with others. Their actions have led to scholarship opportunities for both Keeley and Aidan, and they have inspired other kids to get involved and become interested in science as well. The students included in this book are inspiring role models for our own children, and they show us what is possible when we are open to having our children's interests guide the connections they make online.

Brick Wall, Jellyfish, and Backbone Parents

Several years ago, I was a part of a network of parents who brought author Barbara Coloroso to our school community to talk about parenting and her book *Kids Are Worth It*. I will never forget her talk, as it really resonated with me as a daughter, a mother, and an educator. She spoke about three kinds of parenting styles: the brick wall parent, the jellyfish parent, and the backbone parent.

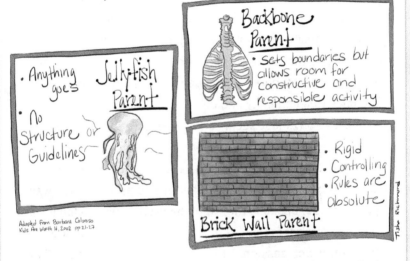

Backbone Parent
• Sets boundaries but allows room for constructive and responsible activity

Jellyfish Parent
• Anything goes
• No Structure or Guidelines

Brick Wall Parent
• Rigid
• Controlling
• Rules are absolute

Adapted from Barbara Coloroso Kids Are Worth It, 2002 pp 21-27

Fishe Richmond

I was raised in a brick wall parent environment. The default setting was NO. Some of my friends had jellyfish parents, and I was so jealous because they could do whatever they wanted. After I saw Coloroso speak, and knowing that brick wall parenting didn't work for me, I strove to be a backbone parent, and I think, for the most part, this worked. I tried hard to allow my kids to make choices, even when they were little: "Would you like to wear this outfit or that outfit?" When my kids got older and they wanted to dye their hair, I said, "It's your hair . . ." (praying they wouldn't choose a color I would have to explain to my parents). Coloroso shared that, as long as a decision doesn't put your child or someone else's child in danger, kids learn from the consequences of making their own choices. Tattoos? Sure. What would you like on your body for the rest of your life? Piercings? OK, if you have thought it through, you can save up your money and get one. (I didn't necessarily volunteer to drive them though.)

For the most part, I felt like I had a handle on this backbone parenting thing—except when it came to technology! I had allowed the media to scare me into rigidity. I set parental controls, and I was absolute about rules that I had set. It is not surprising that my kids engaged in media use behind my back in those early years. On the opposite end of the spectrum, many parents engage in jellyfish parenting when it comes to technology and cell phones, laughing about how kids these days just seem to know all this stuff, not establishing any kind of guidelines for time spent online, or allowing kids to play games rated 18+ at the age of ten. When something goes wrong, these parents jump into brick wall parent mode. Because they don't have strategies to fall back on, they often freak out and ban devices for long periods of time. After one session, I remember a parent saying, "That explains it, so-and-so is such a jellyfish parent!" (And so I want to make it clear that I don't include these descriptors so we have new language with which to judge each other—parenting is tough enough—but that the descriptors remind us of where we are and where we'd like to be. It's definitely a work in progress.)

I think I have finally reached the point where I am a backbone parent when it comes to use of devices. This is not true all the time, and I definitely don't think I've got it all figured out. Alec Couros, a professor of social media and father of four, describes the benefits of being a backbone parent well (although he doesn't use those words). He talks about the importance of connection, and thinking about it in these terms really works for me:

Connection is the term I use over and over. Connection can be about playing with our children, laughing with them, or enjoying time over a good meal. It can be connecting to them while helping them do their homework. It can be connecting with them online through whatever the current app they're using happens to be. It can be connecting with them by posting a photo with them like I just did. It can be connecting with them in the times that they feel sad, angry, or disappointed.[1]

When Should I Give My Child a Cell Phone?

If kids are to explore their interests online, they're going to need access to a device. This leads to the question every parent inevitably has on their mind when they come to a parent talk: When should I give my child a cell phone? (In the next chapter, we will cover the related question of "When is it okay to let my child have a particular app?") Your child will ask you for a phone when most of the other children in their grade have one. They will say, pleadingly, "*Everyone has a phone*," and you may be tempted to repeat what you likely heard your own parents say, "If everyone jumped off a cliff, would you?" From having given a talk to about 250 kids in grades five to eight, I can tell you that almost everyone really did have a phone. I know because I asked. When we moved to teaching remotely, many students did not have another device to access online resources, so many of them used their phones. I don't believe that there are or should be any hard and fast rules for when a child should get a phone. Children mature at different rates, and every family has unique needs. For example, although Sydney got a phone in ninth grade, we gave my daughter Kelsey a phone in seventh grade because her sister was off to a different school and Kelsey would be getting off the bus alone.

Multiple considerations should guide your decision of when to get your child a phone. Devorah Heitner, author of *Screenwise: Helping Kids Thrive (and Survive) in Their Digital World,* lists maturity and independence as factors for deciding if your child is ready. In a *Washington Post* article, Heitner shares the following questions:

- Can they focus in the face of distraction?
- Do they exhibit good judgment?
- How does your child manage social relationships?[2]

Even though we talked about developmental phases in the previous chapter, it is worthwhile to consider that a smartphone is expensive and powerful. Heitner suggests that, if you are already struggling with your child not being able to sit and do their homework or focus on simple tasks, if you have trouble getting them to take care of their belongings, or if your child is already extra sensitive to what peers do or say, they may not be ready for a device. She also poses an important question to consider before purchasing a smartphone: Will you have time to mentor your child?

An organization called Wait Until 8th provides an extremely compelling argument for why parents should wait until at least eighth grade before getting a smartphone.[3] They cite the fact that kids' brains are still growing, and their tagline is "Let kids be kids a little longer." I will often encourage parents to wait if they can. I want you to know, however, that while giving your child a cellphone can expose them to "adult things," it can help them be kids too. A smartphone can be a place to play guessing games (Heads Up), a camera or photo editor, a video conferencing tool, a video creation tool, a science experiment gadget (Google Science Journal), or a music creation tool (GarageBand). As we've seen in the global pandemic, it can be a lifeline for connection. It can also be a powerful way to teach your child self-regulation and responsibility. Keeping your kids young longer is more about our mindset as parents than whether or not they have their own phone.

A good friend and colleague and I had a conversation about waiting longer than other parents before giving in to a cellphone. She told me that she resisted giving her child a phone until well into ninth grade even though she knew that all of the other kids had one. Upon reflection, she recognized that, because so much communication happens through the phone, their family decision impacted her child's ability to socialize. She said she thought she was doing the right thing at the time, but, if she had known how much it would impact her daughter socially, she would have made a different decision. While I am not suggesting you give into peer pressure or make a choice that is not right for your family, you might want to give a second thought to deciding on an absolute date without considering the other factors that are at work in your child's community or friend group. Perhaps several parents can get together and "wait until eighth" together. If your circumstances are such that you give your child a phone at a younger age, consider the positive benefit of having much more of an opportunity to mentor because your kids actually listen to you when they are younger (at least mine did). A good solution (perhaps one you were forced into during the pandemic) is a shared family tablet.

Now what if you've already given your child a smartphone but wish you hadn't? Establishing clear guidelines is a great strategy that can help you regain balance and sanity. Check out this chapter's Try This! section for advice on how to do this.

What Content and How Much Time Online Is Appropriate?

Once upon a time, the American Academy of Pediatrics (AAP) gave parents hard limits on how much time kids should spend online, but their guidelines changed in 2015. A significant change was acknowledging that all screen time is not created equal and that the quality of what kids are doing online is more important than the time they are spending there. Here are their current guidelines:

- Younger than 18 months: Avoid use of screen media other than video-chatting.
- Ages 18 to 24 months: Those who want to introduce digital media should choose high-quality programming and watch it with their children to help them understand what they're seeing.
- Ages 2 to 5 years: Limit screen use to one hour per day of high-quality programs. Parents should co-view media with

children to help them understand what they are seeing and apply it to the world around them.

- Ages 6 and older: Place consistent limits on the time spent using media and the types of media and make sure media does not take the place of adequate sleep, physical activity, and other behaviors essential to health.[4]

These guidelines make sense given what we learned in the previous chapter about cognitive and social development and how device-free zones and times complement some of the biological and emotional needs of children.

The AAP also says to give preference to "high-quality" apps. The fact is, creating apps is a big business. How do you know if an app is educational? There are millions of apps, and as it turns out, very few educational apps are educational on their own. The key, as stated by the AAP policy, is co-viewing and talking about what it is that children are viewing or creating.

For instance, when your child will be interacting with an app on their own so you can get something done, look to avoid the following:

- apps that have ads with mature content;
- apps that are rated higher than your child's age;
- apps that entice your child to pay for extra features (called freemium); and
- apps that collect and possibly sell information (this is usually in the fine print of the privacy guidelines, which many of us just skip over as we press accept).

Talking about apps with other parents is a great idea, and Common Sense Media is an excellent resource for discerning which apps are best because parents have the ability to comment on and review them. Use the search bar to look for the name of an app to see what other parents think about it. If your child is old enough and they are asking for a particular app, ask them why they want the app and what they wish to do with it. This is a great way to discern the value to your child and the skills you think your child will benefit from.

Whatever apps and programming you choose, Dr. Jenny Radesky, lead author of the AAP's policy statement "Media and Young Minds," says, "What's most important is that parents be their child's 'media mentor.'"[5] This means teaching them how to use their device as a tool to create, connect, and learn, and it means being involved.

It is also really important to use language to differentiate what kids are doing online. In the article "Tips and Scripts for Managing Screen Time when School Is Online," Common Sense Media author Caroline Knorr suggests reframing the screen-time conversation using language that defines the activity: "friend time," "down time," "playtime," and "work time." If we name the activity we are emphasizing that the tech is secondary to what they are doing with it.[6]

What Does Parental Involvement Actually Mean?

Parental involvement is repeatedly cited in research studies as one of the most important factors in helping to develop healthy relationships with digital media. One Common Sense Media study states, "Embracing a balanced approach to media and technology, and supporting adult role-modeling, is recommended to prevent problematic media use."[7]

At first, I had a pretty narrow definition of parent involvement. When Sydney was in kindergarten, I became the co-chair for the Parent Council (aka PTA) at my daughter's school, a role I held for a decade. I will never forget going to my first meeting and coming home a little bewildered that I had accepted the position even though I didn't have an ounce of experience. Initially, we met monthly to discuss fundraising and school issues, but then I connected with parent councils from other schools, and together we brought in parenting experts, psychologists, and authors. We made sure that we provided a network for parents to share resources and to come together to ask questions. I learned quickly that I wasn't the only person struggling and that talking to others really helped. Although everything about this experience was positive for me, being a part of your child's parent council is just one example of parent involvement. There are many other ways to be an involved parent.

As I mentioned in the previous section, parents can act as media mentors by modeling balanced media habits themselves, as well as by co-engaging with media; discussing media-related best practices, strategies, and ethical dilemmas; and setting limits around how, when, and where to use media. Alexandra Samuel, a tech writer, researcher, and author of *Work Smarter with Social Media*, has done research that suggests that children of technology limiters, who focus mostly on minimizing their children's use of technology, are most likely to engage in problematic behaviors online, such as posting hostile comments or impersonating others, whereas children of media mentors are much less likely to engage in these types of behaviors.[8] Understanding that adults are role models, parents should be conscious of how they engage with technology and media, given how they want their children to engage with technology and media. If children observe parents being frequently distracted by their phones, they may be more apt to internalize that behavior. Modeling sets an example and establishes a social norm.

But remember, no guilt, no shame. When we know better, we do better, and the best thing is that our kids will be there tomorrow and we can try again.

How Can I Approach Restrictions?

Remember what a brick wall parent looks like? Well, as I mentioned, when I was young, my mom and dad had a default setting: No.

Can I go to the movies? No.

Can I have a friend over? No.

No matter what the question, their immediate answer was always no. Sometimes I was able to persuade them to say yes, but often the no would stand. They restricted my every move when I was young. It wasn't just about a curfew: they timed how long it would take me to get home from school and expected me to be home in that time. I was not allowed to go to the movies or to the mall like most kids. They were, of course, trying to keep me safe, and so much of their stance had to do with cultural factors. My parents were immigrants from Italy, and I was a girl. Although I guess I get it on some level, as an adolescent trying to fit in, it really sucked. I am ashamed to say this, but I ended up lying to them all the time. I took some insane risks, and truth be told, I am surprised that I survived to talk about it with you. Now before you close this book feeling like you can't possibly read another word from someone with an obviously questionable moral code, I want you to consider the words of Aija Mayrock, author of *The Survival Guide to Bullying: Written by a Teen.* She says:

> Today, when I speak to parents and educators, I urge them to recognize that social media is not going anywhere, and stopping your child from using social media is not the answer. My parents did not allow me to use social media in middle school, so I made secret accounts.[9]

It might be easy to say, "Well, that's her personal experience. My child would never go behind my back or create secret accounts." And that may be true. However, when I was doing my master's in curriculum and technology with a focus on social media, I was really interested to read the research of Xianhui Wang and Wanli Xing. In their survey of 270 teens, they found that "parental involvement [had] greater direct influence on online risk than parental restriction."[10]

Let me write that again: parental involvement has greater direct influence on online risk than parental restriction.

Similarly, another study found that the use of parental filters did not reduce online risk. Specifically, they found that there was no statistical link between parental filtering and online risk because of age. In nonacademic language, that means that parents more often apply filters for younger children, and, separately, younger children encounter less risk since they use the internet less.[11] Both studies reinforce what I know to be true based on my own experiences, as well as what I see working with teens every day as an educator and what I have learned by speaking to thousands of parents: a "set it and forget it" approach will not help.

Are restrictions useful when your child is young? Yes, of course. I have links to video tutorials in my chapter resources for this book at jcasatodd.com for how to set up family sharing with an iPhone or an Android phone, as well as how to create a Google SafeSearch and restrict YouTube access. When your kids are young, you can avoid YouTube altogether by choosing KidTube (YouTube app for kids), which has really taken to heart privacy and eliminated ads. When I set limits on our home computer for the girls, they (much) later revealed that, while my husband and I felt secure in the knowledge that we had restricted when and what my kids could access, they had made it their mission to "hack" the system and were on whatever site they wanted, whenever they wanted. Of course, when I knew better, I changed my approach. I know this isn't the answer you are looking for. It would be awesome if there were a magic pill or app that would allow you and your family to have perfect peace of mind, but the reality is that life is messy, and from the mess comes the best learning and the best way to help kids develop critical-thinking and problem-solving skills, as well as resilience, which they will need as they get older.

What about surveillance apps? Nearly every time I talk to parents, someone asks me to recommend one. I always lead with this: I couldn't talk to my parents about anything because I was afraid of them. On the tendency in education to block and ban social media,

Henry Jenkins, danah boyd, and Mimi Ito say, "Blocking sites actually perpetuates risk, as it ensures that many kids will be forced to confront online risks on their own."[12] Today, it is easy to give into the fear and get a surveillance app, but I do not recommend it. This is not just because of my personal experience but because the literature and research out there prove it is a bad idea. According to Tonya Rooney, an early childhood researcher at Australian Catholic University and editor of the book *Surveillance Futures: Social and Ethical Implications of New Technologies for Children and Young People*, "[t]he use of tracking apps can give a message to the child that they cannot be trusted to look out for themselves or to make responsible decisions." She adds that navigating some risk provides "important skills for developing independence and confidence, skills that help guard against risks a child may encounter later in life."[13]

The article that quoted Rooney, "The Case Against Spying on Your Kids with Apps," led me to a research paper, "Safety vs Surveillance: What Children Had to Say about Mobile Apps for Parental Control," which includes excerpts from kids' rating of the apps. Here are a few that stood out to me:

> This app will cause trust issues with your kids. Ever since my dad installed this app, he and I have grown farther apart. If he doesn't trust me enough to use my phone, then why should I trust him?

> Seriously, if you love your kids at all, why don't you try communicating with them instead of buying spyware. What's wrong with you all? And you say we're the generation with communication problems.

> Fantastic. Now my mom is stalking me. I have nothing to hide. You can always just ask to go through my phone. Too invasive and downright disrespectful. Thanks for the trust, Mom.[14]

Ouch.

I am careful not to pass judgment here. Remember, parenting is hard enough without casting judgment. There are likely kids for whom a surveillance app may be necessary to truly keep them safe. If your child has given you much cause to worry or distrust them, then a surveillance app may help until your child gets back on track. This should, however, be a last resort, and if your child requires a surveillance app, you may already be seeking professional help for them.

Henry Jenkins said it best: "Your child needs to know you have their back, but not necessarily that you are looking over their shoulder."[15] He also suggests that kids may actually be safer online than offline. On- or offline, the research points to the need for kids to have their own space to explore. Does this make you uncomfortable? If it does, sit with that discomfort, and be honest with your child about what it is that makes you uncomfortable and why. You may say, "I don't want to prevent you from doing this, but honestly I am so very uncomfortable and worried about something bad happening." The result of the conversation needs to be an action plan moving forward and a check-in from time to time.

Try This! Strategies for Your Media Mentor Toolbox

Backbone parenting

Here are a few tips for being a backbone parent when it comes to device use:

- Co-create family guidelines for cell phone use (see more details below).
- Moderate time spent online versus time spent offline and have conversations about balance.
- Encourage exploration of online communities for creating and connecting (under your guidance).

- Have ongoing conversations about what kids are seeing, learning, and excited about, as well as what they are uncomfortable with or wondering about. Model this by engaging in your own think-aloud about what you are seeing, learning, excited about, uncomfortable with, and wondering about.
- Ask questions and learn about what your kids are learning, seeing, and doing online.
- Model the behavior you would like to see, and admit your own shortcomings and struggles.

Parent guidelines or contracts

In 2012, author, speaker, and founder of iRules Academy Janell Burley Hofmann wrote a letter to her thirteen-year-old son setting up the terms and conditions for him to have a cell phone.[16] Among the rules were that she had to know the password to the phone and her son had to hand it in at night, as well as leave it at home from time to time. One of the rules explicitly states, "Do not send or receive messages of your private parts or anyone else's private parts. Don't laugh. Someday you will be tempted to do this despite your high intelligence. It is risky and could ruin your teenage/college/ adult life." As much as that particular statement might make you uncomfortable, it needs to be said. The end of the letter is significant because Hofmann reminds her son that mistakes will be made and that when that happens, the phone will be taken away and they will start again: "You and I, we are always learning. I am on your team. We are in this together."[17]

The AAP has a great springboard for family guidelines called the Family Media Plan,[18] and although it is very long, many of the prompts are really good. No matter what contract or guidelines you settle upon, it is important to include your child in the discussion by asking: Which of these do you find unreasonable? Which of these do you think you will struggle with the most? Is there anything we should add or take away? That may seem counterintuitive.

In many cases, because you are the parent, you make the decisions. Period. However, including input from your child gives your child co-ownership of the plan and will result in a greater likelihood it will be followed. I have included a template for Family Media Guidelines at jcasatodd.com.

Embrace technology use

Research shows that the most successful strategy is to use technology to help kids navigate online spaces. Alexandra Samuel, author of *Work Smarter with Social Media* says, "It's not our job as parents to put away the phones. It's our job to take out the phones and teach our kids how to use them."[19]

Delay gratification

A famous study known as the marshmallow test seemed to prove that the most successful people were the ones who waited for things. If you are not familiar with the experiment, it worked like this: A marshmallow was placed on a plate in front of a child. The child was told that if they didn't eat it, they would get two marshmallows later. Apparently, when they tracked these child participants into adulthood, the kids who could control themselves during the test were the ones who were more successful in life. These conclusions have since been scrutinized (and even debunked), but there's some truth to the idea that when kids develop skills to wait for things, they are more likely to achieve greater academic competence, healthier weight, effective coping strategies, and more positive relationships with peers. Interestingly, although we talk about this generation as being unable to wait for things, research has shown the opposite to be the case.[20] In parenting terms, what this means is that we may want to consider not saying "yes" to that game or that app. Instead, we can say, "Not yet." We can also delay gratification so they don't immediately get the latest and greatest device, or we can make them work to earn it. Chores around the house are a good way to work for a device or anything else kids really want, since, believe it or not, research also points to the fact that successful people are ones who did chores as children.

Alternatives to smartphones

If you are going to wait until eighth, a family tablet is a great way to get your family's feet wet. You can remove all apps that you are not comfortable with, and because it stays in a central place in your home, you can be involved in what your child is reading, creating, or playing. As companies try to capitalize on parents' wishes to delay technology use by their children, more and more products aim to meet those needs. If you use Apple products, an iPad will allow you to use family sharing features. iPads are, however, quite expensive, and other tablets work well too. Some people have also gone back to flip phones. When you go to the chapter resources at jencasatodd.com, you will notice I have updated a list with current products on the market.

A digital playground

It may be useful to think of the online world the same way you think of a physical playground. When my kids were young, we made the trek to the local playground daily (mostly because they were up so dang early that I needed to do something with them!). I didn't necessarily expect them to be well-behaved or that the children around them would be well-behaved, but I'd taught them to be kind, respectful, empathetic, and patient. I accompanied them to the park on their playdates to ensure that, if there were any issues, I could help guide them. I played with them, and I was quick to celebrate when they shared, took turns, and played nicely, but I also stood far enough away that they could deal with conflict on their own.

When my kids entered school, I had faith that their teachers would assume the playground supervisor role, that they would respond encouragingly when all was well and intervene and help problem solve when needed, and that if there were any issues, they would communicate them with me. I expected the teachers to respond. As my kids got older, I stood back more and only intervened when necessary. Gradually, I let them venture out on their own.

Friend and educator Daniel La Gamba[21] created an illustration after a conversation we had about digital playgrounds and the importance of reaffirming the positive and redirecting the negative, both in the classroom and as parents. Think about the online world as a physical playground where we can help kids develop the skills they need to navigate online and offline situations and conflict.

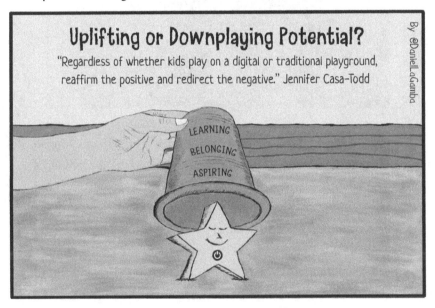

Uplifting or Downplaying Potential?

"Regardless of whether kids play on a digital or traditional playground, reaffirm the positive and redirect the negative." Jennifer Casa-Todd

By @DanielLaGamba

Let's Talk about It

- Does your child feel safe, loved, and connected? How do you know?
- How might you show interest in what your child is creating or playing online?
- Who in your life might you share strategies and struggles with?

WIZARD AND WONDER CHOPRA

Ayush Chopra was a thirteen-year-old student at Ahlcon International School in India when he started his journey as a young advocate for the United Nations Sustainable Development Goals (SDGs). Ayush has been recognized with the highest accolade a young person can achieve for social action or humanitarian efforts, the Diana Award. The Diana Award is given in memory of Diana, Princess of Wales, and it's the longest-running award given to outstanding young people for selflessly creating and sustaining positive social change.

Ayush is the Founder of SDGs for Children, a unique platform for children across the globe to connect, create, and collaborate for a better and sustainable world. He is also one of the pioneer Indian ambassadors for the TeachSDGs project initiated by the Global Goals Educator Task Force, a worldwide network of teachers established in 2017. He is the only student ambassador among the first group of over one hundred distinguished global educators. He has also been a student ambassador for various other global projects like SOS4Love Project, the Climate Action Project, the Goals Project, SocioStory, The Kindness Project, and more. Ayush was appointed as the Ariel Foundation International's youth ambassador and their youth representative at the United Nations. When he was fifteen years old, he was invited to represent India as the Indian youth ambassador at the 14th Annual International Human Rights Summit. His speech on human rights at the UN received a standing ovation from the distinguished gathering.

Ayush is the author of *Shaping A Fairer World with SDGs and Human Rights*. The book is the culmination of his experiences, initiatives, and intense involvement in social transformation. Using engaging design and artwork, the book communicates information about SDGs and human rights with engaging design and artwork. It is now being used as a daily reference guide for teaching the United Nations Sustainable Development Goals in many classrooms across the world. Ayush also has his own podcast, *Shaping A Fairer World*. The podcast is an attempt to connect educators, students, and parents together and to share voices and unheard stories across the globe. Ayush believes that "nothing can stand in the way of the power of voices calling for CHANGE."

Ananya Chopra is Ayush's sister, a twelve-year-old student known as Wonder Ananya on digital platforms. She's the CKO (Chief Kids Officer) of SDGs for Children, also a youth ambassador of the Ariel Foundation International, and author of *Save Our Planet*. Ananya is passionate about working for the United Nations Sustainable Development Goals. She started her journey with SDGs at Ahlcon International School when she was in fifth grade. She has participated in many global and local campaigns. Ananya got inspired to work for social causes and inequalities through her school and her brother. Ananya is also passionate about sports. She has won cash prizes and trophies at state and provincial squash tournaments in India and Canada. She believes sport is a powerful tool for achieving sustainable development.

She recently published the book *Know Your Rights or Have No Rights*. In this book, Ananya shares about the UN Convention on the Rights of the Child (UNCRC). Ananya believes that there is no age limit for dreaming big. If we work hard and act on our dreams daily, no one can stop us from making them true. She encourages her friends to live their dreams!

Both Wizard Ayush and Wonder Ananya are guided by their parents and global educators. They have created amazing relationships with many mentors on social media who guide and support their work. Their journey on social media and in the real world is an example of how a perfect balance between the two can not only help create a great learning platform but also can create ripples for other children to follow. They believe that #WorldChangersAreNoisy and are busy in #ShapingAFairerWorld with their small actions.

VALERIE LEWIS

assistant principal and parent of two, Atlanta, Georgia

My now twelve-year-old created a Snapchat account, and I nearly lost my mind. I was in a state of panic because I know the messages on Snapchat are designed to disappear and cannot be retrieved. We had already had issues with him watching and repeating adult content from YouTube videos back when he was in the third or fourth grade, and it was scary to know that Snapchat could be an inappropriate or even unsafe portal to communicate with friends and strangers. My immediate response was that he should delete his account because I had not given him permission and he was underage, but being an educator with a love for technology, I was conflicted. I wanted my son to be able to share with me what he was doing online and create accounts with our blessing, but when I paused to think further, I realized that in order to create a Snapchat account, he must have had an email address to link to it. What was happening? Oh boy—we were in deep.

We had a conversation about all of the accounts he had created and why he felt it necessary to have them. While this was still unsettling, we established rules about posting videos and sharing private information like addresses and family members' names. We talked about how we don't truly know if people are who they may appear to be online and about the dangers of navigating a virtual world. We took a break from devices for a few months and slowly reintroduced them, using them only on weekends and charging them in my room at night.

When my son requested me as a friend on Snapchat and started sending me little messages here and there, I embraced the opportunity to connect with him in a way he felt comfortable with. This was a window into his world, and had I scared him away through scolding and finger wagging, I might not have had this front-row seat.

I quickly got over my remaining anxiety about Snapchat one day after we had gotten rid of our home phone line. I was having some regrets about removing it until my son put Snapchat to good use by calling my phone from the tablet while I was out to tell me that his younger brother had not been feeling well and was throwing up. I must admit that, until he called my cell phone, I had no idea Snapchat had a free call feature embedded. However, using that feature, I was able to give him directions on how to best support his brother in the short time it took until I pulled into the driveway at home. In that moment, I recognized that responsible use of social media had opened an avenue of safety and connectedness that was not only a great way to relate to my son in his world but could be used for communication in ways that could potentially save a life. The fear of the bad had been overshadowed by the good that could result.

3

Social Media

Amid the many news headlines in recent years, you must have noticed that, increasingly, younger people are using social media as a platform for change. In 2019, Greta Thunberg mobilized millions of young people to fight for climate action. After the 2018 school shooting in Parkland, Florida, several teens strategically leveraged social media to draw attention to and have conversations about gun control. The #BlackLivesMatter movement mobilized countless young people all over the world, including my own children, who felt compelled to share information in a way I hadn't seen them do before. Regardless of where you sit on any of these issues, what is abundantly clear is that social media allows for anyone at any age to have a voice.

While preparing for a keynote presentation in Halifax, Nova Scotia, I learned about a teen, Stella Bowles, who had discovered that sewage was being dumped into a local waterway, and she leveraged Facebook to put a stop to this. She convinced three levels of government to pledge over $15 million to clean up the river in her community.[1] Social media allows for a new reality: kids can propel change. I have seen kids establish social media campaigns and create petitions through change.org to make a change. In my book, *Social LEADia*, I quote from Ishita Katyal's TED Talk titled "Be Whoever You Want at Any Age": "I believe age is just a number. I believe anyone is capable of great actions and can touch the lives of others, regardless of his or her age."[2] She spoke these words at eleven years old.

When the world literally stopped during the COVID-19 pandemic, we also saw artists, authors, zoos, museums, and celebrities take to YouTube, Instagram, and Facebook Live to help people cope, reach out to those in need, and brighten our spirits. At my own school, our students used social media to stay connected and to lift each other up.

Famed personal-development author and speaker Wayne Dyer says, "If you change the way you look at things, the things you look at change."[3] This has been my motto in recent years. Let's think about one of the most common social media platforms we use: YouTube. It can be a place to be entertained, to spread hate, or to be inspired. It can also be an incredible place to learn. My husband finished our entire basement by watching YouTube videos. There are so many kids who are using YouTube to share their voices and talents with the world. My friend Brian Costello shared a YouTube video created by his nephew, Jonathan, called "Stuttering: In My Own Voice." In it, Jonathan shares what it feels like to have a stutter and how we can be more kind and supportive of someone who has a stutter.

When a young woman at my school named Elizabeth came to my desk crying because she needed me to write a letter to give to her lawyer so she could stay in the country, I immediately thought about how I might amplify her voice so we could get more people to send letters. She was really nervous about sharing her story and her worries about being deported, but she agreed to record it. My heart broke as I watched her record and rerecord herself. When she was ready, we went into a classroom where the English teacher, a compassionate and passionate educator, was willing to interrupt her regularly scheduled lesson to let Elizabeth present her video and answer questions and to allow the students, if they were moved to do so, to write a letter on Elizabeth's behalf.

When I got home, my daughter asked, "Who is Elizabeth?" The question took me aback. I didn't understand how she knew about Elizabeth, as we hadn't talked about her yet. What I soon realized was that even though I had left the video unlisted, it was already going viral. Within two days, it had over seven thousand views. We got hundreds of letters. But more importantly, a parent who learned about Elizabeth's story was a lawyer, and they agreed to take on Elizabeth's case.

That spring, I co-organized our graduation ceremony, and it was a blur. The one moment of clarity was watching Elizabeth walk across that stage. Because of the power of social media, she was able to stay in the country and graduate. Two years later, her brother graduated as well, and they are both still here now. When I share that story, people reveal their own stories about the positive power of social media, and for a few minutes, all those headlines that serve up fear are forgotten.

What Is Social Media and What Are the Risks?

Social media is considered "[a form]" of electronic communication (such as websites for social networking and microblogging) through which users create online communities to share information, ideas, personal messages, and other content."[4] In and of itself, social media can be seen as neutral. The fact is, through social media we now have access to people and ideas we never would have had access to before. Most social media platforms rely on community guidelines (rules about how to engage) with some mechanisms for checking content. Now don't get me wrong: social media companies definitely have to clean up their acts, a fact that became glaringly clear with the connection between social media and the US Capitol riots in January 2021. As you know, with any community, one negative person or group of people can ruin it for everyone. This is why social media gets such a bad rap. But here's the reality: Social media can be used to build people up or tear them down. It can be used to share information or misinformation. It's *you* that makes the difference.

My philosophy with my own children and my stance in my book *Social LEADia* is that your experience will be, in part, determined by who you follow and what you share. For example, I follow inspirational student digital leaders who are using social media to learn and share learning, to celebrate and empower others, and to make a positive difference in the world. I follow educators who do the same and who encourage their students to do likewise. Rather than always emphasizing what *not* to do, we need to spend as much (if not more) time showing kids how powerful social media can be when used in appropriate and positive ways. Case in point: this posting from a fifth-grade teacher, Donnie Piercey, who wanted to share an inspirational poem written by one of his students with as many people as possible.

donnie @mrpiercEy · Dec 6
One of my fifth grade boys wrote this poem today. He asked me to share it with as many people as possible:

#edchat

> You Can Do Anything
> By-E▒▒▒▒▒▒
> It never matters how much you look
> Never let others hold you back
> If they ever laugh and say you can't do it
> Just believe and you'll prove it
> Don't be afraid to do what you can
> Just keep doing it hand to hand

♡ 9   ↻ 44   ♥ 180   ↑ W

Creating versus consuming

When we reference quality versus quantity, the difference between the time spent online creating versus the time spent online consuming is key. For example, watching YouTube videos is considered consuming media, but when kids are making videos to distribute on YouTube, they are engaging skills that will help them in the future. I have often said that we need to spend more time creating than consuming. And while this is true, Dr. Henry Jenkins adds that not every child has to make media for the rest of their lives, no more than any child would collect stamps their whole lives. Kids can contribute to the digital world not just by creating their own media but also by recirculating media with commentary. Kids' media creation and consumption will likely ebb and flow based on their interests and passions. The fact remains, however, that "[w]hen kids make media, it changes the way they look at media."[5]

The Dangers of Social Media

The headlines that focus on all of the negatives are heart-wrenching and scary. Let's face it, as parents our natural instinct is to protect our children and keep them safe. On any given day, social media directly results in obesity, anxiety, depression, and eating disorders, as well as the threat of online predators, identity theft, and cyberbullying.

A white paper called "Online Harms" provided an overview of the many terrible things that can happen to children online. Something that struck me in the research paper, however, was this:

> Most children have a positive experience online, using the internet for social networking and connecting with peers, as well as to access educational resources, information, and entertainment. The internet opens up new opportunities for learning, performance, creativity and expression.[6]

It stands to reason that your child will fall under the "most children" category. The media focuses on the "other" instances. When we unpack the research cited in the paper (and many other research papers), we can see that social media and technology are a part of the problem, but often many other factors impact the negative and tragic outcomes.

We can never totally protect our children from the possible negatives. We had a neighbor who rented out a room in their house. The tenant gave me the creeps. There was something about him that really scared me. I remember reminding Kelsey about our secret password and about never getting in the car with strangers. But then, as he said hello to her, I realized I had to remind her not to get into the car with acquaintances either. Then I was paranoid that she wouldn't know what that really meant, so I told her she could only get in the car with a relative or with specific family friends. It came to a point where I didn't want her playing outside. My husband thought I was being utterly ridiculous. Nothing ever happened. For all I know, that man was a perfectly harmless and friendly neighbor. The point of this story is that we can't let the fear of what might happen to our children prevent us from letting our kids experience life, but we do need to be aware of possible dangers and equip our kids with safeguards and strategies to keep them safe.

When our children are playing an online game or interacting on the day's popular social media platform, we often imagine that the person they are corresponding with will lure them and kidnap them or make them a victim by asking for nude photos. Is this a possibility? Of course, it is. And our most vulnerable children fall victim to this. Remember Maslow's hierarchy? A young person who does not feel secure or feels like they are lacking belonging and acceptance will fall prey to someone who is being overly kind and attentive to them online. If, however, we shift our thinking to realize that the internet may not be as scary as it is portrayed, we can allow the panic to be replaced with common sense.

Likewise, we can't be panicked by the idea that one false move online could ruin your child's life forever. We've seen the headlines: people's lives and jobs become at risk when they do or say the wrong thing online. Can this happen to your child? Possibly, but that is why mentoring your child and helping them navigate digital drama on their own is a good thing. We need to emphasize the permanence of the online world, encourage them to think critically before they post, and model the very important delete button. The problem with being ultra-fearful all the time is that it usually doesn't match your child's reality. Though negative headlines might dominate, research studies point to the evidence of positive impacts of technology.

Because most of the time kids spend online is in positive situations, they see you, with your fears and worries, as being "extra" (a word my children call me all the time, which means "extreme"). Here's the thing: I don't want my children to be fearful in spurts and starts; I want them to be mindful every day. To make that happen, here are some of the important conversations we need to have (which you may want to incorporate in your Family Media Guidelines):

- We always keep personal information (address, banking, passwords) private.
- We always share if we have any intention of meeting someone we met online in person, and we always do so together.
- We always send appropriate photos, never a nude, even when we are pressured to do so.
- We always get each other's opinions if we are unsure if something is real.
- We engage in kind, respectful language toward people of all cultures, races, and genders.
- After we post something, we check our tone and content to make sure it fits with our values, and we delete it as soon as possible if it doesn't.
- And most important, when we accidentally or unintentionally make a mistake, we immediately have a conversation about it to try to solve the problem.

This last point is important because it tells your child that they are going to make mistakes and that your role as a parent or guardian is to help them solve the problem. You will also notice that these guidelines are written positively. This is because the brain better recognizes what it should do, rather than what not to do. We need to equip our kids with strategies to have a healthy skepticism (on- and offline), and our kids need to know they can depend on us if something goes wrong.

Social Media and Mental Health

When I was young, I suspected that everyone was having parties and not inviting me, but I did not know that for sure until my peers came back to school to talk about it. The feeling of loneliness and isolation was almost unbearable. Today, kids know with absolute certainty that their peers are having fun without them because they can see it unfold on social media. I can't tell you how many times I had to sit and listen to my daughters cry, heartbroken because their friends were having fun without them or hadn't invited them to something that everyone else was at. Linking depression and anxiety with social media thus seems to be logical.

Yet there is much research that counteracts this claim. Researchers at the University of Kansas found that there was no difference in well-being between a group of participants who abstained from using social media and those who didn't.[7] Another report by The Royal Society for Public Health found that reading blogs or watching vlogs on personal health issues helped young people improve their knowledge and understanding, prompted them to access health services, and enabled them to better explain their own health issues or make better choices. It also noted that young people are increasingly turning to social media as a means of emotional support to prevent and address mental health issues.[8] And in the United States, Common Sense Media found that "[a]cross every measure in our survey, teens are more likely to say that social media has a positive rather than a negative effect on how they feel."[9]

I know what you are thinking: *This can't be.* Almost every headline tells us that social media is linked to depression and general lack of well-being. And for some people, it may very well impact them negatively, especially if they are already struggling with issues of belonging or self-esteem. Many of the headlines we read are also examples of extremes. When you read the entire article, there is almost always a paragraph (near the very end) that cautions us about blaming social media. In fact, there are many reasons that today's teens are more likely than ever to be depressed and anxious: intense competition, high expectations, perfectionism, worries about getting into preferred colleges, climate change, school violence, and on and on.

What Should I Know about the Apps My Kids Want?

Help! My kid wants a YouTube channel!

The more I get invited to speak to parents, the more I get this common question: "My child wants a YouTube channel. What should I do?" YouTube is the most common search engine behind Google, and in many cases, YouTubers are today's celebrities to our kids. In fact, I often share that my daughters will buy products on the recommendation of their favorite YouTubers (which brings up an entirely different discussion about the need to help kids to understand media literacy and, in particular, techniques YouTubers are using to sell products, which I talk about later in this chapter).

When a child wishes for a YouTube channel, it is often because they are influenced by YouTube stardom. So as a parent, what should you do? First, know that YouTube isn't inherently bad for your child. Consider the YouTube mission:

> We believe that everyone deserves to have a voice, and that the world is a better place when we listen, share and build community through our stories. Our values are based on four essential freedoms that define who we are: freedom of expression, freedom of opportunity, freedom of information and the freedom to belong.[10]

You may be thinking (like I did) that just because YouTube has positive intentions, it doesn't mean it's right for your child. It is important to note that YouTube is meant for kids aged thirteen and older. This means, that when your eight-year-old asks, it is perfectly reasonable for you to say, "You are too young." KidsTube is an app that is far better for your younger child. It may be a good idea to keep them on that app as long as you can. YouTube also allows for parent sharing, which means that you may have some control over your child's experience. (A YouTube guide is included in the chapters resources at jcasatodd.com.)

But this book is all about digital leadership, so consider eleven-year-old Louie, who has had a YouTube channel since he was ten, where he shares his art with the world. His mom, Diana, has mentored him every step of the way by helping him with scripts and encouraging and supporting his creativity. Starting a YouTube channel should be a joint venture, and your child will need your mentorship and support to create the channel and continuously along the way. If you or another caring adult or older sibling will not have the time to help, it may be a good idea to embark on a YouTube channel journey another time.

Next, it is extremely important that you ask your child why they want a YouTube channel and what they would like to share with the world.

When my daughter was quite young, she wanted to create movies starring her American Girl doll. My nephew wanted to create a channel to help people play *Minecraft* more effectively. Olivia Van Ledtje uses Vimeo rather than YouTube to share her favorite books and reviews of them. She, too, is mentored by her mom, Cynthia Merrill. In the time I have known Olivia, she has gone from reviewing a few books by authors to meeting many authors and becoming a keynote speaker and author! She created content that people found valuable but that most importantly fueled her own passions.

Here are some questions you can ask while considering your child's request:

- What does your child wish to share?
- What are they passionate or knowledgeable about?
- Why do they want to share their voice with the world?

Then, do some research. Before creating the channel, consider having a look at the YouTubers your child is watching and ask them these questions:

- What is interesting about the message?
- What do you like about this?
- What would you do differently?

It may be worthwhile to check out some educational videos together while asking the above questions. If your child has a favorite, go with that. Otherwise, TED-Ed Student Talks, Scholastic, SciShow, National Geographic Kids, Discovery Channel, SunnyKids TV, and It's Okay to Be Smart are a great place to start. I have curated a list, which can be found in the chapter resources at jcasatodd.com.

With over 2 billion logged-in monthly YouTube users 81 percent of whom are fifteen- to twenty-five-year-olds in the United States,[11] you need to know that just because your child chooses to create a YouTube channel, it doesn't mean anyone will necessarily watch. Lots of kids start a YouTube channel, but if their motivation is YouTube stardom, they usually don't last very long. We don't want our children to be obsessed with views and subscribers anyway. Instead, help your child realize that a YouTube channel should primarily be for their own creative outlet.

Ethan Duncan, a high school student, with whom I shared a stage at the International Society for Technology in Education conference, revealed that he created a YouTube channel to dispel the myth that boys can't be dancers. In his talk, he shared that having a YouTube channel helped him learn how to communicate on a global scale, how to make the world better, and how to make an impact. In a follow-up YouTube video a few weeks later, he reflected on the fact that many adults who attended the conference seemed obsessed with how many subscribers he had. His message is an important one to emphasize. At first, it may be useful to share videos and the channel with family members and family friends to build momentum and support, but a slow and steady start is not only inevitable, but preferable, and conversations around fame and subscribers are necessary. For older kids, or for your own reference, YouTube has created a certification program that will take you through the process of how to start a YouTube channel with a business in mind.

When it comes to YouTube, one of the biggest fears parents have is that a YouTube channel will open up the floodgates for hurtful or hateful comments. Consider, however, that responding to negative comments (as long as they aren't extreme) is an excellent way to build resilience in your children. Dr. Alex Russell, a clinical psychologist and author of *Drop the Worry Ball,* says that mentoring your child on YouTube can be about teaching your child how to respond to positive and negative comments, a skill that may serve them well as they get older. Still, you definitely don't want to open your child up to mean and hurtful comments that may diminish their self-confidence. Luckily, YouTube has many options for this. You can disallow comments altogether, but I suggest you moderate the comments instead. You can add filters to ensure mean comments get held for review or you can hold all comments for review, then allow the positive or neutral ones and delete the negative ones. I have included a link at jcasatodd.com that will walk you through this.

Instagram

Almost every news outlet and celebrity has an Instagram account, and although the demographics are changing (the more adults that move to a platform, the more kids will run in the opposite direction—see Facebook as a clear example of this), it is projected that the number of active Instagram users in the United States will reach 12.5 million by 2023.[12] From the first iteration to today, Instagram has evolved to have Stories, which disappear within twenty-four hours; the option to go Live if you are doing something cool; make Reels, for short creative videos; and use Instagram TV for longer videos.

I will never forget the day in 2017 when my daughter used the (at-the-time) brand-new Instagram Live feature. Because I follow her on this platform, I was notified that she was going Live, and I jumped in. Her response and the response from her friends: "Oh my gosh, your mom is on here." Then a shuffle, panic, and the livestream video ended. I don't know that she had an awareness of audience at the time. I used it as an opportunity for her to teach me about Live video on Instagram, which she was only too excited to do. The reality in my household is that my kids no longer use the platform with any kind of regularity, and when they do, it is to post a very strategic and "beautiful" pic. When I've asked about why this is, I've learned that not oversharing on Instagram is an unwritten rule. Instagram users are primarily between the ages of eighteen and thirty-four,[13] so this might not be an app your kids are begging to get. If, however, many of their friends are there, having a conversation about the "unwritten rules for posting" will give you great insight into what your child values and understands about the platform.

Snapchat

On the other hand, Snapchat is currently hugely popular with young people. Snapchat has 310.7 million monthly active users, with 90 percent of Snapchat users between thirteen and twenty-four years old.[14] This is somewhat misleading, however, because the minimum age requirement for Snapchat is thirteen, but tons of kids lie about their age to gain access. Snapchat came into our household when my girls were fifteen and thirteen years old, respectively. When it first came out, headlines about sexting paralyzed me with fear. I kept imagining that my mostly well-behaved and respectful kids would suddenly start sending nudes of themselves to boys and that this would ruin their reputations and their lives.

When they wanted the app, they did what they always have to do when they would like to download a new social media app (a condition born of the fact that we pay for their data plan and phone):

1. Tell us why they want it.
2. Tell us what they want to do with it.

3. Tell us what the privacy terms are and how they will be safe using this app.

At the time, I figured I knew as much as I needed to know about the app, and I allowed my girls to get it. They have been on it ever since. In fact, I would say that Snapchat is the app my girls continue to use most frequently, and my youngest daughter now uses the Group feature in Snapchat to organize group projects for her university courses.

When I was completing a course on social media in education, I thought quite a bit about intergenerational digital literacy and the rights of children using digital media, and I realized that I really had little idea how or why my girls (who were fifteen and thirteen at the time) used Snapchat to communicate, how this app worked, or what its forms, conventions, and etiquette are.

CEO Evan Spiegel describes Snapchat's mission: "We're building a photo app that doesn't conform to unrealistic notions of beauty or perfection but rather creates a space to be funny, honest, or whatever else you might feel like at the moment you take and share a snap."[15] There is no liking, sharing, or commenting and very little editing functionality. You can determine how long you want your snap to last (between one and ten seconds or until the person taps off the snap), and then they presumably disappear. Having said that, snaps stay on their own servers for at least thirty days.

Initially, there was quite a bit of eye rolling from my daughters about how little I knew about the app. The girls proceeded to tell me about my story and how it can stay up to twenty-four hours but anything else disappears after only a few seconds and that I can time my snaps to last for up to ten seconds. They were showing me some of their friends' stories and helped me to create a story.

I asked about how you could get into trouble here. That's when my teens proceeded to tell me that that would happen only if you were "stupid enough to post a nude or something." Then the person on the receiving end could screenshot the image as a way of keeping it. "We're not that stupid, mom."

What became very clear, very quickly was why they liked to communicate with their friends using this medium. Unlike the posed shots (selfies) filling Instagram, in Snapchat, you could be goofy. We posted the

- triple chin shot,
- close-up nostril shot,
- crazy eye shot, and
- big toe shot.

We laughed hysterically. The next day, the girls sent me a few snaps with their friends, and we agreed that I wouldn't try to be friends with their friends (even though I think I'm a cool mom), that I would only use Snapchat with them . . . or with my own friends. Because of my Snapchat experience with my girls, I learned the following lessons:

- Adults often mistakenly presume kids are using social media for negative purposes.
- Kids really appreciate and enjoy teaching adults what they know.
- Kids are savvier about protecting themselves online than we sometimes give them credit for (although we need to reinforce privacy and protection whenever we can).
- Kids value (as they always have) friendships and communicating with friends, and their smartphones help them to do that.
- Taking an interest in something that is important to them is very validating and rewarding—for everyone.

Kids need a space where they can have private conversations and have fun. As adults, we should know about these spaces but not necessarily encroach on them. Soon after my girls taught me about

Snapchat, I created a Snapchat group with my own friends. The sole purpose of the group is to sing (bad) karaoke to one another. My secret purpose? To stay on top of this app that my kids use with such regularity. It is by doing this that I learned about Snap Map.

Snap Map is a geo-location setting that will allow users to see where other users are. This freaked me out a little. OK, a lot. I immediately started asking my kids to explain the idea of Snap Map. *WHY WOULD YOU WANT ANYONE TO KNOW EXACTLY WHERE YOU ARE?!* The all-caps was my inner voice, which screamed this in a panic-stricken accusatory tone; my outer voice took the form of an "I wonder" statement. My daughters explained that you can go into Ghost Mode, which means no one can see you and that you can actually have much control over who can see your location and who can't. If you share to Our Story you appear on the Snap Map for anyone in the world to see. The idea behind this is that if you are on a hike on Mount Everest, at a sports event, or experiencing something amazing, you can share that with the world. From my mom point of view, it just felt creepy, and thus, we needed to revisit our tech family guidelines. My girls had to set their location to Ghost Mode. On the other hand, I have heard of families who use the location feature to know where their older children are (for example, if they are out at a party).

I also noticed that there was a way to lock images called "For Your Eyes Only." Surely that could not be a good thing. I was able to ask my girls about the feature with a naïve question and an "I wonder" statement: "I noticed this feature, For Your Eyes Only. Can you show me how it works? I wonder what people might use it for?"

I know all of this seems very complicated, but this is why mentoring matters so much. We won't know what questions to ask if we don't stay involved, talk to others, and continue to keep the lines of communication open.

There is a link to more info about Snapchat Map with the chapter resources for this book at jcasatodd.com. It might be even better to ask your child about it.

TikTok

I am sure you have heard of TikTok. During the COVID-19 pandemic, this music video creation app became very popular as a way to break the monotony of quarantine. While browsing your own social media feeds, watching late night shows, or viewing the news, you may have seen videos of parents pouring wine in their cereal (a direct result of remote learning) or parents and kids dancing together in their backyards, likely with the distinctive musical note TikTok logo in the corner. I first learned about TikTok's popularity when my daughter would have her friends over and spend hours rehearsing and recording dance numbers. I have to say I loved it! She would often complain about how some of her friends would just hang out on their phones when they came over, but this hanging out on the phone is entirely different.

As with any social media site, there is potential for awesome as well as for danger. The platform in and of itself is not the problem, but there can be some seriously mature and inappropriate content on it. Parents I have talked to reveal that kids as young as nine and ten years old have discovered the app and are pressuring their parents to get it.

One of the most important things for parents to know about TikTok is to go to the Privacy and Safety settings to control who sees the content you create, who can send you messages, whether you want to filter comments, and so on. Whenever I am getting ready to present a workshop for parents, I search TikTok and download videos I find interesting that are set to public to use in my presentations. Think about that for a moment: I can have a video your child created on my phone right now, even though I don't know you or your child. If what your child has posted can inspire others, that's not a bad thing.

No matter what your choices are regarding the safety settings, you must, as a parent, continue to stay involved. Your kids may want to switch to public because they want to get more likes. This requires a conversation. Are they determining their self worth by likes? Or are they strong and assertive? Are they a competitive dancer who wants to use TikTok for a portfolio of their work? More and more teens at my school are talking about being "TikTok famous," a term given to someone who garners a large number of likes.

Here are a few important things to know about TikTok:

- At the time of writing, there was a Digital Wellbeing tab that allows a parent to manage screen time and put the app in Restricted Mode, which means the content they can access shouldn't contain mature content. However, the password you create is only valid for thirty days and then needs to be reset. In April 2020, TikTok also added a Family Pairing feature to its Digital Wellbeing tab. This feature allows you to link your account with your child's and then set a limit on their watch time, exclude content that isn't suitable, and limit who can send messages.[16]
- The app has mature content (profanity, sexuality), as well as creative and wholesome content. Many songs used in TikTok videos may also have explicit content. There are trending hashtags on the home page that may include challenges. Challenges (sometimes sponsored by companies) can be altruistic, funny, or totally inappropriate.
- A Report tab can be used to let the company know of inappropriate content. TikTok has come under fire for not doing enough to protect the personal information of children. As of 2020, they have apparently committed to prioritizing children's safety, including through internet safety seminars.[17]

They also have some great educational video tutorials that range from how to keep your information private to how to delete and block users.

- What you see on your feed is completely determined by the videos you like (TikTok utilizes algorithms to determine what you would like to view). My students in our school book club have "BookTok," that is, their feed is filled with people sharing their favorite books. My husband's feed is primarily DIY videos. Kelsey's feed has many health professionals as she was recently diagnosed with a medical condition (more about critical thinking and credible sources later). My friend's daughter who wants to be a medical doctor watches someone perform autopsies!

When Is the Right Time for Social Media?

Related to the question of *which* social media tools are safest, the question I get asked most often is *when* kids should be allowed to access them. When your child says, "But Mom, *everyone* has Snapchat" (or TikTok or whatever the latest and greatest app is), that may very well be true. This is because although most platforms have a minimum age requirement, many kids just put in a different age so they can access the app. One of the ways to circumvent this is to have a frank conversation with your child about why certain apps have a minimum age. It is important to note that most apps set their minimum age requirement at thirteen, not so much because of inappropriate or mature content but because this is the age under which the Children's Online Privacy Protection Rule cites it is illegal to collect personal information.[18]

With the age-old understanding that sex sells and with many of a platform's older users clicking on such content, mature content that is often inappropriate for young users can often be found at the top of the Explore (Instagram), Discover (Snapchat), and For You (TikTok, YouTube) pages, making the simple act of navigating to a platform's home page a risk for kids. One strategy to avoid exposure is for kids to use their actual birthdate when signing up for apps; the algorithms for the platform will typically ensure that the targeted ads and content they get will be based on their age. But, quite simply, if you don't want your child to be exposed to this content at all, wait as long as possible to allow the app. I encourage you to attempt to sign up for the app with your child using their birthday. That way, your child can witness that they are indeed too young to be on the app. You then may agree to create an account with your own email and thus share it with your child. Family sharing is available on many apps, so check the settings for this option. A shared account will allow you to be involved, to learn more about the app, and to ask your child good questions. Once on the platform, be sure to suggest wholesome organizations and positive role models knowing that the experience of social media is about who you follow and any platform can be used creatively and positively.

How Do I Protect My Child from Fake and Misleading News?

One day, my children came home and said, "Mom, the Great Barrier Reef is dead. You guys killed it, and now there won't be any fish as of 2050." I responded with, "Wow! Where did you get that information?" They said, "It's trending on Twitter." So, of course, I asked them to show me, and although it had been trending during the school day, it certainly wasn't when we looked together. When they proceeded to delve into the topic further (our rule of thumb is three credible sources), they admitted they hadn't checked other sources.

As a teacher-librarian, I feel it is my job to help students with media literacy, which includes asking critical questions of sources. According to research out of Stanford University, middle schoolers and high schoolers have difficulty understanding the credibility of websites and posts, and school alone is not doing enough to help. The spread of misinformation is a huge problem.

When I try to determine whether an image is real or fake, for example, I ask myself these questions:

- Is the account verified (usually a blue checkmark beside the user's name), or is the author one who is considered an expert?
- Is the image plausible and realistic?
- If I do a "reverse image search" on Google, will I find the pictures featured in other sources?
- If I do a Google search for the account, do legitimate news sources come up?
- What is the purpose of this media—what is it trying to persuade me to know or do?

When I first started teaching, I was thrown into a twelfth-grade media studies class and I had no idea what I was doing. My saving grace? The media triangle. You see, whether I was having the kids look at newspaper articles, films, or commercials, we could use the lens of the media triangle to understand the media messages.

When social media came on the scene, I recognized that the media triangle still fit. In fact, so many problematic behaviors and consequences happen because kids don't understand how media works. The only problem is that teachers are sometimes afraid to bring social media into the classroom. If we aren't helping kids to understand social media in school and kids are on social media, then we as parents need to help in that area. I have since brought the media triangle into my parent talks.

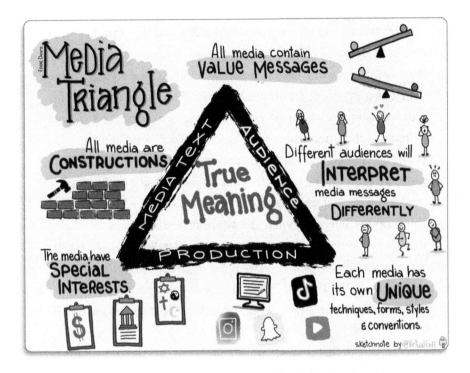

The three legs of the triangle consist of media text, audience, and production, reflecting the interplay of what the message is, who is receiving the message, and the platform used to share the message. So whether I am talking about a Facebook post, blog, Instagram post, TikTok video, tweet (Twitter), or snap (Snapchat), the media triangle is applicable.

Media Is a Construct

Most importantly, we need to remember and remind our kids that media is a construct: someone is creating what we hear or view for a certain purpose. This is especially important when it comes to body image. Even twenty-five years ago when I was teaching that media class, people were concerned with the images in magazines and how the "perfect body" was being portrayed. Now those advertisements sit on your personal device. When I know and remember that media is a construct, I can help my children realize that they should always be a little skeptical of the *perfect* anything. It is constructed to look that way. My favorite media lesson was about food styling. Those delicious burgers or that beautiful turkey? Spray-painted! When my kids are comparing themselves to someone else's perfect life, I need to remind them that there may have been an awful catfight right before the perfect post or that hundreds of pictures may have been taken before a person perfectly curates one. When I read an article by Australian Instagram celebrity Essena O'Neill, who apparently "blew up the internet" when she swore off social media, admitting that every picture and every post was completely fake and that she was never truly happy, that is what I brought up at the dinner table that night. O'Neill states, "The concept of faking a 'perfect' life on social media has been around almost as long as social media itself."[19]

I would extend that to say that the concept of faking a perfect life or body has been around as long as media itself. Have you seen some of those "perfect wife, perfect life" kind of images from the 1950s? There is a great video that I always invite parents to share with their kids in which actors show an Instagram post compared to "real life." My favorite is the "beach scene," which is actually a picture taken of someone in a pile of sand at a construction site while he was wearing his flip-flops and bathing suit!

Your child needs to hear the idea that media is a construct often enough that every time they look at a post or picture or news headline, they are skeptical and wonder why it was put together that way.

Media Has Special Interests

That Snapchat streak that makes your child so desperate to not break it? That's a brilliant construction to keep your kid coming back time and time again. That YouTuber who your child feels like they know intimately? They look into the camera and speak directly to your child; they create suspense or entertainment and construct a relationship and a story for their viewers.[20] Autoplay on YouTube is also designed to ensure that your child gets lost in YouTube rabbit holes for hours on end.

This is because the other important thing to remember about the media triangle is that media is a business. That game, that Snapchat streak, the longing for kids to get on the For You page on TikTok all exist so you will use the product and watch their ads. People make money based on how many subscribers they have on YouTube and how long they actually watch. Twitter? Facebook? Instagram? We are the ones who are creating the content while not earning one single cent. And while we use these platforms, companies collect cookies (bits of information we leave as we post, search, and reply) so they can create targeted ads for us, which make them money.

Media Contains Value Messages

Another important part of the media triangle is understanding that media contains value messages and different audiences interpret messages differently. The reason that intelligent people can be duped by fake news is that we tend to interpret things based on what we value. Media is often constructed by people who want to persuade us of a certain opinion. We also have to understand that we interpret any message with bias. Our brain, as it tries to make sense of the world, is hardwired to recognize what it already knows. This is called confirmation bias. So that article about social media destroying the world? Many won't read to the end or even notice any alternative perspective because the headline and first few paragraphs confirm their thinking. To interrupt this, we need to first acknowledge our biases, and then we need to ask ourselves a few very important critical literacy questions: What is the purpose of this message—that is, what is it trying to persuade me to do? Whose voice is missing?

ANAHIT HAKOBYAN

I am a student leader for the Global Education Student Chat, an initiative that brings students together from all over the world and allows them to share their ideas and opinions in a safe digital space. As an individual who is passionate about inspiring younger students, I was delighted to join the group as a leader. Before GlobalEdSsChat, I refrained from using social media. Social media usage is usually discouraged for young people by parents who are worried about the negative effects it can have on their children. However, GlobalEdSsChat has highlighted the importance of social media in education and as a tool for social change. Students discuss topics each month such as online privacy, innovation, mental health and well-being, cultural awareness, and more. Social media is a powerful way to deliver your message to others and leave a positive digital footprint.

While learning in the classroom is important, a forum to discuss real-world issues and topics has been an invaluable gift. Interacting and networking with a variety of people has allowed me to discover my passion and purpose in life. It is very difficult to know what you are passionate about if you have never wandered outside of your comfort zone. In the past, I would dread public speaking, but when I pushed myself to try new things, I found my purpose. In addition to speaking on YouTube Live, I have contributed to blogs and have been able to eloquently express myself. Being part of a virtual community is essential for young people. It gives us a sense of belonging and fosters creativity and the drive to strive for greatness.

None of this is new. I remember doing a comparison with three front-page articles with my students about twenty years ago. We compared the picture, the headline, and the first paragraph to understand the underlying message that each carefully constructed piece was trying to express. What is new is the extent to which we have access to information.

You may look at that TikTok or YouTube star and find them less than amusing, but your child, who is trying to find their own place in the world, is going to be impacted very differently. Adults and kids don't always share the same values. While you may be completely unaffected by the number of likes your post gets, your child may well be pinning their identity and self-esteem on the number of likes they are getting.

While you may be wondering what this has to do with digital leadership, I can assure you that the students whom I have met who have the healthiest relationship with media and who are positive role models for others are ones who understand how media works and can distance themselves from it when needed and leverage it positively when they want. Media literacy shouldn't just be taught in classrooms; with all of the media around us in its varying forms, it is important for us as parents to reinforce a healthy skepticism for our kids around everything.

How Can I Help My Child Develop a Positive Online Presence?

A digital footprint is the trail of data you create when using the internet. This includes websites, emails, and, of course, information you submit to online services, including social media.[21] When I talk to tenth graders in careers classes, I share the idea that everyone's digital presence can be considered positive, negative, or neutral. I ask them to do the following:

1. Identify three characteristics or personality traits you would like someone to know about you.
2. Google yourself. If nothing comes up on Google, go into your social media accounts and have a look at what you have posted or liked.
3. What are three characteristics or personality traits someone who doesn't know you would assume about you solely based on what people would see online?
4. Does your online presence reflect who you are as a person? Is it reflective of your values? If it is different, did you do this on purpose? What would an employer think?

Amazing conversations have come out of this exercise. Many kids have either a negative or neutral digital presence. I encourage kids to talk to their parents about the advantages and disadvantages of using their real names. One of the things I do in my role at school is help kids to think about how to use social media to be career ready.

How Can My Child Use Social Media for Their Future?

As a mom, I know I emphasized the importance of protecting my child's identity online. Yet, when I have conversations about career planning in tenth grade, I recognize that just like my child's email, which had to change from a fun childish username to a more professional one, at some point it is advantageous for your child's real full name to be used online for the purpose of career readiness. Like it or not, we live in a world where employers Google prospective candidates. According to one source, 54 percent of employers have rejected candidates based on their social media profiles.[22] Another source claims that 70 percent of recruiters have rejected candidates based on what they have seen online and that 92 percent of recruiters use social media to find high-quality candidates.[23] Maybe this strikes you as awful, but regardless of how we feel about it, this is the way it is. In addition to the exercise reflecting on your digital presence I shared in the previous section, think about what you are posting about your child and how you are creating a digital footprint for your child. That really funny tantrum that seemed totally appropriate to post may well show up when an employer is searching for them, and although that might not impact them, your child should consent to what it posted online about them. It is always a good idea to get permission before posting and to be thoughtful about what you are posting. By doing this, you are also modeling a culture of permission: other kids should not be posting pics of your child without their consent and vice versa.

There is also the decision to have your child use their actual name for an account they would be proud to share with an employer. This may be a conversation for when they enter high school. Think about it in these terms: if a newspaper were sharing information about your child's accomplishments, wouldn't they identify your child by first and last name? Sharing positive things online can be a way to showcase the talents and interests of your child. Even if they choose not to post any original content, I encourage my high school students to follow colleges and universities they are considering, as well as organizations and careers they are interested in pursuing.

One of the ways kids are getting around the idea that they need to have a professional identity is to create a "finsta" or "spam" account (especially on Instagram). An article I read discussed kids creating fake accounts that their parents or grandparents would approve of, while having a fake account to "be themselves." My younger daughter had a joint spam account with some friends where she felt like she could "be herself." I did not feel strongly that she should delete this account because when we talked about it she was very open about why she and her friends created it. Together, we looked and and talked about the content in there from time to time. I considered it a win that she talked openly with me about it. It also led to a fascinating conversation that made me realize that kids try on different digital identities, which is perfectly natural.

Olivia Van Ledtje often challenges adults, saying that online and offline are the same and we need to stop talking about them as if they are different. Olivia is unknowingly making the same argument as Nathan Jurgenson, a social media theorist, who says that digital dualism (the idea that online and offline are separate realities) is a fallacy and that, instead, online and offline are increasingly enmeshed.[24] Still, some kids do see their online and offline identities as very different. One student I interviewed for my master's thesis told me that she didn't know who she wanted to be online yet. This really made me think about how kids are making choices about what to reveal to the world. If you recognize a really big difference between how your child is portraying themselves online and their offline self, you may want to have a conversation about why. What they say will likely give you great insight into what they are struggling with in terms of their identity, or it may surprise you in a good way too.

Try This! Strategies for Your Social Media Toolbox

Pay attention to who you follow

As I already mentioned, social media is about who you follow, and your experience will be a direct result of that. When I follow an account, no matter what the social media platform, I am given suggestions as to who else to follow. Suggestions are generated by algorithms. Twitter, for example, looks at your location, your existing contacts, and the accounts you already follow.[25] This is where following accounts who inspire and uplift really helps.

You likely have told your kids that they should only follow people they actually know, which is generally good advice, but I would say that if you encourage your child to follow kids such as Joshua's

Heart, Khloe Kares, Mia's Boxes of Love, and Brae's Brown Bags, you and your kids can see other kids making a difference in the world. For a daily dose of positivity, follow accounts like Ellen, Brad Montague, and Uplift (Facebook). If I follow organizations about marine life because I am interested in pursuing a career in marine biology or if I follow NASA, what I see on my social media feed is going to be more about learning than if I only follow celebrities. It is worthwhile to have a conversation with your child that isn't simply about making sure they don't follow strangers, but also about which "good strangers" will help them to learn, be inspired, and network. Want to be a doctor? You can follow the most prestigious medical schools in the world with the click of a button. Does your child want to be a mechanic? They may already be following lots of accounts that showcase cars, but how about car companies from around the world and innovative practices in other countries? In this way, they will have a good answer if they are asked at a job interview (as you will recall my daughter being asked), "What social media are you on and what will I learn about you if I go there?" They are curating a professional presence that they can readily share with employers.

We will talk more about how making decisions about who to follow may also protect your child from negativity in the last chapter, but your child's interest and passions are what ultimately will drive these decisions. I have curated a list of people and organizations to follow with the chapter resources at jcasatodd.com, and I'd love for you to suggest other inspiring accounts in the Raising Digital Leaders Facebook group or by tagging @RaisingDigitalLeaders on Instagram.

Get a group and play

My advice to parents whose kids are on a tool: gather some friends, get the tool, and play with it. I can hear you saying, "Are you crazy? Who has the time?" I know you have laundry and lunches and work that you have brought home that you need to get to, but we need to engage in some of these spaces in the same way that we would spend time being interested in the offline activities our children are into. I remember watching synchronized swimming videos when my daughter was a synchronized swimmer and watching the entire *Heartland* series (you likely haven't heard of it for a reason) because my daughter was in love with horses. Now I occasionally use TikTok to create short videos, and I have my bad karaoke group that my friends and I use to learn about Snapchat.

Balance

At first, your child will be obsessed with all things related to their YouTube channel or the social media account they are allowed to use. This is natural and not in and of itself a cause for concern (consider that my friend's daughter spent hours and hours editing videos and then went to university to become a filmmaker and is now in that career). It is important that even before you embark on this journey, you decide what is an appropriate amount of time to spend on the channel or online. The American Academy of Pediatrics stresses that quality is more important than quantity when it comes to screen time, so when your child is creating, this is better than consuming (watching videos). Dr. Henry Jenkins speaks of balance not as a day-to-day thing but something to consider over time. That is, if your child is spending hours creating and curating for their channel because it's their latest interest, that is completely normal— just as they might be into Pokémon or Harry Potter or go through an obsession with magic. Nonetheless, it is important that you talk to your child explicitly about getting fresh air, exercise, and a good night's sleep.

Combat perfectionism by becoming a healthy striver

The Counseling & Mental Health Center at the University of Texas makes the distinction between being a perfectionist and a healthy striver, which is an important distinction to be aware of and to reinforce on- and offline.[26] Anxiety and fear can create energy, and healthy criticism can lead to resilience. However, being too preoccupied with a fear of failure can lead to the negative consequences of perfectionism. One of the ways to strike this balance is to reinforce and celebrate effort. Don't just post the best achievements of your child online, but also make a habit of posting something positive related to skills your child is learning or effort your child is making during a regular game or riding lesson or practice. Regularly reinforce the fact that social media is a construct, and debunk the myth that the "perfect" life portrayed on social media is real. Another strategy suggested by experts: empathize but don't try to fix. Stress and anxiety are normal and necessary. Empathize by saying something like, "I can see how frustrated you are about this," but don't jump in to help. Instead ask, "What are your strategies to help you get over this?" So often my daughters (or students) will say, "I have no idea what my strategies are." In that case, I pull out the "I wonder" statements until one resonates.

Here are a couple of examples:

- It seems like all of your friends got a major part in the school play and it must be really disappointing that you are a part of the chorus. I wonder if this is a good thing? If maybe you will still get to be a part of this awesome experience but will also have time for other things? How are you going to make the best of this situation?
- It must feel really yucky that many of your friends posted that they got an A on that test when you didn't do very well. I didn't do well in that subject either, but I used a tapping

strategy to help me remember. I wonder if that might help you too.

Modeling

When I was doing my master's, I learned about American psychologist Albert Bandura's theory of observational learning. Basically, it says that children watch, learn, and are impacted by the behavior they see and often imitate it.[27] *Gulp.*

When you hear people say that kids are like sponges, they are essentially referring to this theory of social learning. Of course, gossiping is an easy habit to fall into, but if you are frequently gossiping in front of your child, this behavior becomes normalized. However, if your children see you go out of your way to compliment people or be kind to them, that is the behavior that becomes normalized.

Because misinformation is such a huge issue, we need to ensure that we are not reposting articles or information that isn't credible or true. It's also where a "think aloud" or an "I Wonder" statement can come in handy:

"This article's title seems like clickbait (purposely trying to attract my attention). I wonder how much truth is in here. I am definitely not going to share until I check it out."

"I wonder if I can find three credible resources that also say this."

"I have to make sure I read other sides to this story, because I think I have a bias when it comes to this topic."

A great poster that I have used in my classroom for many years calls upon us to THINK before we post.

- T—Is it true?
- H—Is it helpful?
- I—Is it Inspiring?
- N—Is it necessary?
- K—Is it kind?[28]

It is mostly because of the theory of observational learning that I curate lists of inspiring student (digital) leaders who are using social media to learn and share learning, to celebrate others or support a cause that is important to them, or to be a positive influence on others. The more our kids see what appropriate use of technology and social media looks like, the more easily they will recognize what is inappropriate. The lists available at jcasatodd.com are a great starting point, but your child's interests are an even better starting point. Encourage your child to follow organizations and people that are informative and inspiring, not just entertaining.

Let's Talk about It

- What is one thing that resonated with you in this chapter?
- Is it time for a social media cleanse? Are you following people and accounts that uplift you or bring you down? Take control of who you surround yourself with.
- Can you identify some of the skills your child is demonstrating on social media?
- How can you help your child understand how media works?

NICHOLAS CLAYTON

special education teacher, director of Mia's Boxes of Love, dad of Mia, Apple Valley, California

Mia's Boxes of Love, Inc. was born when five-year-old Mia gathered a box full of her toys and told us she wanted to give it to homeless children. She came up with the name and logo design for her organization herself. We contacted a local shelter to find out what was needed. Mia wasted no time! Her first outreach was a backpack drive. We were able to donate over a dozen backpacks, along with supplies and an additional five hundred dollars, with the help of schools and social media.

At the same time, Mia was a YouTube fanatic, and she loved to watch Kid President's videos. When she heard about his #Socktober campaign, she decided to work on a campaign at her own school. She reached out to family on Facebook and received donations for socks from relatives. As parents, we followed Mia's lead. It is a rare occasion when you hear about children leading their parents, but our inspiration for helping to create the project, which is now a nonprofit, was the drive Mia had to help others. We are in the mindset as parents that it is important she know to "do awesome" with the gift of our fortunate circumstance as people whose basic needs are met. We gave Mia guidelines for what she needed to do to get the word out using social media platforms, and we continue to guide her to make sure she is aware of how important her work is to people. Now we have a family charity that over the past five years has provided more than forty thousand pairs of socks and other donations to our local charities/homeless shelters. And Mia recently added published author to her repertoire with her picture book *Mia's Boxes of Love* in Socktober of 2019!

LOUIE DACOSTA

Louie DaCosta is a sixth grader from New Jersey who lives with his parents; his younger sister, Ellie; and his dog, Lola. He enjoys playing defense for his soccer team and playing the violin. But his real passion is drawing. Starting at the young age of three, he began sketching his signature butterfly for family members.

Whenever he wanted to know how to draw something, he would watch a tutorial on YouTube. Kids always told him that his drawings were awesome. His friends would say things like "That's really incredible!" or "How did you draw that?" One day, it hit him: "The pictures I draw are really good! Maybe, I can start a YouTube channel to teach kids how to draw."

He asked his mom if he could start a YouTube channel. His mother thought this would be a great way to teach him how to use social media in a positive way. When he first started out, his mom was very hands-on behind the camera, filming, coaching, and troubleshooting when Louie created his videos. She taught him how to edit his video clips in iMovie and post to YouTube. Eventually, she handed over the different aspects of creating his tutorials when he demonstrated he could do it on his own. Currently, Louie mainly relies on his mom as a sounding board for his monthly themed sketch ideas and to troubleshoot any issues if he gets stuck. Louie dost most of the filming, editing, and posting of his videos on his own.

It wasn't easy in the beginning, but Louie studied and learned from a good friend who was sharing her love of books with the world through short video clips called "LivBits." Having Olivia Van Ledtje as a friend and mentor helped him to realize he needed a plan for his idea of creating art tutorials on YouTube.

He also took classes through YouTube Academy with his mom to learn how to manage his channel.

Over time, he learned that if you are going to create a channel, you should choose to share something you're passionate about. When he makes his videos, Louie is always excited and enjoys himself. He believes that if you are passionate about a topic, it doesn't feel like work. He understands that he has an audience of peers, family, and also adults, like teachers, who follow his channel, so he is mindful about what he shares.

Gaming

Whether you have a two-year-old, a twelve-year-old, or a twenty-two-year-old, gaming is a topic that every parent will likely tackle at some point. Gaming is a force today. *Fortnite* for example, at its height had around 200 million users. For comparison, the game's users amount to just over five times the population of my entire country of Canada at the time I am writing this. One article tried to make the point stick with the headline, "Fortnite Bests Russia and Japan to Become World's 8th Most-Populated Place" (with the population of Russia at 142 million and Japan at 126 million).[1] In November 2020 *Among Us* a game many used as a way to connect with others during the global pandemic, took the world by storm with 300 million active players.[2] While middle-aged men seem to be the most consistent game players, you've got to look at those numbers and realize your game-induced family tension is shared by families all around you. In my household, both my daughters and my husband are avid game players. I am not a gamer, and all the gaming makes me crazy! I have literally yelled at all of them (separately and collectively) to stop playing, to pay attention to me, and to turn off the film we are watching if they are just going to play a game anyway. These haven't been my proudest or most flattering momma/wife moments. Yet I am not alone. Even in the library, a few of my colleagues will not allow kids to go on the computers at school to play games. However, thanks to research studies I have read, I have really had a change of heart and mind about gaming.

Are Video Games Really Bad for My Child?

One of the questions parents often ask me is whether their kids should play video games and, if so, for how long. The media again has had an impact on what we think about video games. Headlines regularly say that violent video games make us more violent and desensitize us to violence, impact our ability to pay attention, and make our eyesight worse. Is this just technophobia, or are these claims based on science? What is fact and what is fiction when it comes to video games? The problem is, this is tricky, and what you find out will depend on what you read (are you noticing a trend here?). I'm going to share some of the research I have found that may help you make a decision that is right for your family.

Douglas Gentile, a developmental psychologist at Iowa State University, says, "Media violence is one risk factor for aggression. It's not the biggest, it's also not the smallest, but it's worth paying attention to."[3] Christopher Ferguson, a psychologist at Stetson University in Florida, has published papers questioning the link between violent video games and aggression. Ferguson argues that the degree to which video game use increases aggression is so small as to be essentially meaningless.[4] Other research does link violence in video games to lack of guilt when violent video games are played over prolonged periods of time. But, again, the links are very minimal. Kids who play violent video games do not tend to become serial killers or mass murderers when they grow up.

Richard Davidson, professor of psychology and psychiatry at University of Wisconsin–Madison, created a game designed to increase empathy. Research headed by him revealed that "in as few as two weeks, kids who played a video game designed to train empathy showed greater connectivity in brain networks related to empathy and perspective taking."[5] You may be surprised to learn that more and more games are being created to address problems in society.

Daphne Bavelier, a brain scientist and professor at the University of Geneva, shares a powerful TED Talk, "Your Brain on Video Games," in which she says, "[I]n reasonable doses . . . those action-packed shooter games have quite powerful effects and positive effects on many different aspects of our behavior."[6] Bavelier addresses a few common myths about gaming. The first one is that playing video games makes your eyesight worse. Her research concluded that people who spent five, ten, or even fifteen hours per week gaming had better eyesight than those who don't play. First, they were "able to resolve small detail amidst clutter" (being able to read the fine print on a prescription rather than using magnifier glasses). They were also better able to resolve different levels of gray. Using the example of driving in a fog, Bavelier says, "That makes a difference between seeing the car in front of you and avoiding the accident, or getting into an accident." Her team concluded that when it comes to action video games, screen time doesn't make your eyesight worse, and in fact, they are trying to leverage video games to help improve eyesight in patients with low vision.

On a different level, gaming can be quite social. In March 2020, when we were given stay-at-home orders related to the COVID-19 pandemic, my daughter Kelsey put together a PowerPoint presentation (not the first one in her lifetime—when your parents are both teachers your best strategy is to create a professional presentation outlining your arguments) sharing why we should get a PS4. Her strongest point? It would help with connecting with her friends. I understood how social she is (she's like her momma) and how social distancing would be really tough for her. As a nongamer, I did not understand her desire for the PS4 specifically, but what I did get was the chatting and laughing and strategizing. It was the most normal she felt through all of it. We watched closely whether she would rather spend time in the game than in person, and she did spend quite a few late nights playing, but agreeing to get that device was a good family decision.

How Much Time Is Appropriate and How Can I Spot Addiction?

My local Parent Network (a collection of PTA representatives from about twelve neighboring schools) organized a parent night that consisted of a film, followed by a panel discussion between me, a local police officer and her daughter, and the cofounder of Newmarket Bully-Free Alliance. The film ended with a scientist who had done extensive studies that consisted of playing flashing lights and sounds, such as those you would see in a video game, for lab rats, which led to the determination that they caused irrevocable brain damage. There was a collective intake of breath in the audience from parents who, of course, had kids that played video games at home. The whole time I was watching, I was aware of the point of view of the film and what it was trying to persuade me to think and do. I also thought about the strategic placement of that particular scene at the end. And the lights and sounds the rats were being exposed to? Constant and persistent.

Luckily, I had the media triangle on my side to help unpack what was going on here, and I was able to share my critique as part of the panel discussion. That old expression, "Everything in moderation," is true for online gaming as well. You may recall that the American

Academy of Pediatrics does not give any specific time limits for how much time your child should spend online, and I'm sorry to say there wasn't a separate section that gave limits for online gaming. The AAP guidelines are to set consistent limits and ensure that time online doesn't impede sleep or physical exercise.

The problem with gaming is that there are so many qualities that can make your child (or you) completely lose track of time. Let's go back to the media triangle and Maslow's hierarchy for a minute. Your child may be struggling in school or in social situations in their physical world, but in a video game, they can choose whatever avatar they want and can overcome obstacles to feel success. In education, we often try to emulate the hard but fun work video games create for their users. Games are constructed to keep you coming back. They make their money by making you come back, and because your child is a hero in this world, they *want* to come back.

In moderation, playing video games is fun and has some great brain benefits. In excessive amounts, they can be destructive. In 2018, the World Health Organization recognized something called internet gaming disorder, a condition that resembles addiction to drugs or alcohol: "craving, impaired control, priority given to gaming over other activities and a [continuation to escalate] despite negative consequences."[7] The Child Mind Institute does give a specific research-based recommendation for how much time kids should be allowed to spend gaming. They say that up to two hours a day does not seem especially harmful, whereas additional time can be associated with mental, social, and emotional impairments.[8] Common Sense Media suggests that behaviors such as mood changes, failing grades, increasing bills, and lack of human interaction may warrant a talk with a pediatrician, noting that these are also the same indicators of depression.[9]

Virtual reality games

Virtual reality games (characterized by a headset and complete immersion inside a game that allows the gamer to feel like they are actually in the game world) may cause dizziness if used in excess. Again, there are no set time guidelines and not a great deal of research out there right now to indicate the long-term effects of using virtual reality on the adolescent brain. Experts do advocate moderation. Excessive use of virtual reality can cause headaches because images in a virtual reality headset seem far away but are, in fact, close to the user's eyes, which can confuse the brain.[10] Common Sense Media's study on the impact of virtual reality on children suggests that children (as young as four to six years old) interact with virtual characters in a similar way to how they would interact with them in their physical world. As a result, they recommend parents understand the powerful influence these virtual characters can have and ensure they interact with positive characters.[11]

I use virtual reality in my classroom to bring kids into places and situations they would never really encounter in their lives. My purpose is to create empathy and inspire perspective taking. For example, one virtual reality video I have taught with is called *Clouds over Sidra* and takes us into a refugee camp that Sidra shows us around. I've asked students to think about what might help Sidra have a better life. In another virtual reality film, we follow a thirteen-year-old girl on her journey to get fresh water in her village. A valid question you might ask yourself when allowing content for your child is, "Would this be something I would like my child to experience in their physical world?"[12] If virtual reality is your reality (pardon the pun), you may want to read the entire research report by Common Sense Media (I've put it in the resources for this chapter at jcasatodd.com).

How Can I Keep My Child Safe Online?

A common concern for parents is that the seemingly nice child playing with your child is actually a forty-year-old pedophile or human trafficker trying to lure your child. Is this possible? I will never lie to you: it is. Laura Higgins is a British child-safety veteran hired by Roblox in January 2019 as its director of digital civility. Her job is to learn from these kinds of problems and prevent activities that could harm young players. Although she is tasked with ensuring the safety of players, she admits, "It's an age-old thing: if people have bad intentions toward children, they're going to gravitate toward where the children are. We're constantly reviewing the tools that we have, and looking at ways to improve them."[13]

Chat capability in games generally exists for players to communicate and strategize with each other. It often is very social, but at the same time, opens up your child to strangers online, no matter what the popular game of the day is. This is true for games as well as chat platforms like Discord. Video chat features can give complete strangers a real-time view of your home. Almost every video game has security measures and controls built in to protect children. For example, Roblox, a popular gaming platform, has launched a website called For Parents, which explains safety tools "from algorithms blocking swearwords and names and addresses in text chats, to its reporting system for inappropriate chat or content. There's even an algorithm detecting whether players' avatars are wearing 'appropriate attire.'"[14] A quick YouTube or Google search will lead you to a given game's respective safety features. Having said that, if your nine-year-old is playing a game with an 18+ age rating, it may be less likely to have such features, as there is an assumption that an adult would be able to make their own safety decisions. The Try This! section of this chapter has some additional tips for managing concerns about online gaming. But let's not get bogged down by the negatives. That online chat feature is a great place for your child to learn skills which are actually transferable to the workplace.

How Can Gaming Benefit My Child in the Future?

In his TED Talk "The Transformative Power of Video Games," Herman Narula talks about the economic impact of video games:

> Right now, thousands of people have full-time jobs in gaming. Soon, it will be millions of people. Wherever there's a mobile phone, there will be a job. An opportunity for something that is creative and rich and gives you an income, no matter what country you're in, no matter what skills or opportunities you might think you have. Probably the first dollar most kids born today make might be in a game. That will be the new paper route, that will be the new opportunity for an income at the earliest time in your life.[15]

Just like my friend's daughter whose passion for film editing led her to a career in film, your avid gamer may potentially get into game development, marketing, or design as a career.

Josh Feinsilber, who was a high school student when I interviewed him for my *Social LEADia* podcast last year, created an interactive game called *GimKit* as a school project. He combined a few existing educational games that teachers used for review and added competitive strategic game elements that he felt these educational games were missing. When I interviewed him, the platform had newly launched, and as I write this book today, Josh now runs *GimKit* full time as a business with a co-owner. Imagine my surprise when a friend of mine told me she had an interview for a job with a new game-based company and Josh, the CEO and a new graduate, was interviewing her! This is the world we live in today: opportunities abound for young people that we never had before.

Even if your child never goes into gaming as a career, online games provide important skills that may lead to good habits in the workplace. "There are plenty of soft skills that gamers can utilize in a professional setting, such as teamwork, problem solving and strategic planning,"[16] says Ryan Gardner, a regional director with the recruiting agency Hays.

Digital entrepreneur and business consultant Mia Bennett says that we need to stop thinking of gaming as a pursuit of teenage boys and instead look at it as an opportunity to build skills, including such meta-skills as how to learn, creative thinking, and experimentation.[17]

I have met several kids who have YouTube channels that help other kids with strategies, and I've met other students who are excited about coding and creating their own games. Gabe Howard, who I highlight in *Social LEADia*, is a young man who uses social media to connect with others who might mentor him in game development, and his mom led him to Twitter chats specific to game-based learning. One of my students who helps me run the Coding Club at school will often ask me to look at his code to help him figure out what is wrong. I look at it completely bewildered: even though I run the club, coding does not come easily to me. When I couldn't help him, he got into an online community on Discord, and found a college student who was able to figure out where he was going wrong with his code. My momma instinct first kicked in: Do your parents know you are online? Did this "college student" ask you any personal questions? In the end, I recognized that my student had found a mentor for his passion and skills beyond anything I could offer. He was practicing the skill of networking.

Harvard Graduate School of Education professor Chris Dede says that collaborating face to face is a necessary skill, but, increasingly, students need to graduate with tools that will allow them to successfully collaborate online. We certainly saw this with the sudden move to virtual meetings, schooling, and life as we know it during the global COVID-19 pandemic that forced us to limit our in-person contact. Thus, while online gaming chats can be filled with graphic and inappropriate language or negativity, they can also give kids an opportunity to collaborate online.[18] Online games can foster literacy (the ability to read and write and understand the world). If we recognize some of these skills, we can help our kids make the links to careers or other aspects of their life where they might use resiliency, leadership, and collaboration.

E-sports

In recent years, there has been a movement to bring electronic sports (e-sports) into classrooms across North America and Europe. One day, a group of students brought in a game console and plugged it into the library computer and engaged in a competitive soccer match. I was close to shutting it down. What would an administrator say if they walked in and saw kids playing that game instead of studying? Yet my Library Learning Commons was already filled with games that I bring in and promote. Would I be a hypocrite if I forbade e-sports? This is what prompted me to learn more about e-sports, a form of competitive video gaming with multiple players battling against each other, usually in teams. Their matches are often streamed live to millions of young fans.[19]

I was interested to learn that, in some of the research, e-sports are compared to professional gambling. I had no idea (although based on the media triangle, I should have) that e-sports were such a business and that people actually made their living from playing competitively. Apparently over 380 million people worldwide watch e-sports, and tournaments attract crowds that rival traditional sports games.[20] When we were young, our career aspirations included way more traditional pathways, and if you would have said, "Someday, people will earn lots of money by playing computer games," I would have thought you were crazy! Yet, as a little girl, I watched hockey with my dad, and later I watched it with my husband, who watches every sport in the universe. It only makes sense that, with our evolution to a more tech-driven world, e-sports would develop into a possible career path—and a very lucrative one, with revenues exceeding $1 billion in 2019.[21]

When a young person missed school to play hockey or basketball, I remember hoping the student had a back-up plan because it was so hard to get into the NHL or NBA. There are similar obstacles to becoming successful in e-sports, but somehow the credibility of e-sports is lost on us. This, friends, is a very legitimate thing with careers, including content creators and entrepreneurs. You can even go to the popular ESPN website and get all of the latest updates. And while we imagine e-sports to encourage obesity, research suggests that, even though e-sports are so different from court and field and track games, they can be physical, demanding dexterity and coordination, as well as visual acuity and mental focus, quick reflexes, and coordination.[22]

Josh "CitrusEmpire" Leighton-Laing, a content creator, e-sport moderator, and freelance graphic designer, shares his story about the way in which e-sports allowed him to escape the reality of his anxiety and depression. He says, "We get to live, and relate to stories and characters, or struggles with teams on a daily basis instead of having a self-imposed weight drag us into the dark depths of our own psyches. It allows us to connect to people just like us."[23]

Try This! Strategies for Your Gaming Toolbox

Play games with your kids

Jordan Shapiro, author of *The New Childhood,* advises that playing video games with your kids can ensure a stronger relationship with them and help them deal with or avoid problematic use. Playing video games today is also about collaborating with multiple players. Your child will be in a room where they have access to other players who are playing the same game, including both kids their age and adults. By playing games with your kids, you can learn what to ask them, understand how the games they play and the streaming platforms they are using (like Discord or Twitch) work. They will also feel like you are genuinely involved in a world they care about.

Use a timer

Establish rules around how much time is reasonable to spend playing games. Let me describe a frequently occurring scenario. See if it sounds familiar.

You tell your child they can play games for a few minutes before dinner. Then dinner is ready, but the table is not set. You are frantically trying to get dinner on the table, and there is no sign of your child who had agreed to only play for a few minutes. A yelling match occurs.

Using an external timer works well for a couple of reasons. First, it marks a time that you have agreed to. Next, there is an external signal to stop playing—one that is not *you*. This is called the third point strategy, and it is an effective way to avoid conflict. When your child is frustrated, you just point at where the annoying beep is coming from. We use our kitchen timer, but investing in an inexpensive timer that you can bring closer to your child as it continues to beep can be very helpful too.

Establish a nighttime routine that does not include video games

I remember when the very first *Call of Duty* came out. My high school students were literally asleep in my class (I like to think I am a pretty engaging teacher). And still, all these years later, I am having conversations with my students about how the latest *Call of Duty* is keeping them awake until the wee hours of the night. If your child has access to video games in their bedroom, they may play all night because there isn't an external reason (you) to stop. Some sleep research speaks to how it's difficult to fall asleep when your brain has been activated by playing games. Thus, it's important to establish family rules, like having some downtime before bed that does not include technology.

Follow age restriction guidelines

The age restrictions set out by companies are there for a reason. It is important to be honest with our kids when we explain why we are uncomfortable with purchasing a game that is mature for our nine- or eleven-year-olds. I know this is tricky. Many parents have shared that when their kids are allowed to go to a friend's house, those friends' parents don't abide by the same rules. A few ideas to tackle this:

- Admit that every household has different rules and that our rules work for the values we have as a family.
- Get together with a few friends and establish similar rules.
- Give it a try and co-play with your child. If indeed your child is the only one who doesn't have this game, consider the advice given in the social media chapter and determine whether or not this may socially isolate your child. You may then insist that you can only play together so you can address mature content together.

I wonder/think aloud

Again, thinking aloud, asking naïve questions, or using "I wonder" statements will reinforce positive behaviors and skills and give you a good sense of how savvy your child is when it comes safety. Here are a couple of examples:

- "I wonder how we can set up the computer in our house so that the person I am playing against can't really see anything that identifies our house?"
- "I can't believe how skilled you are at anticipating what others are going to do. I need to develop that skill more at work."
- "I wonder if this person is really a kid. They don't seem to be using language that kids use."
- "I really like how that player is talking strategy. What do you all do if someone is asking questions not about the game?"
- "Wow, I am so amazed by your perseverance. You pick yourself up and keep trying. That is a skill you are going to need in life, buddy. Good for you!"
- "I am so impressed by the strategy talk in the chat. How'd you learn how to do that so well?"
- "We have spent more time playing games today than we have done anything else. We need to do something physical."

Let's Talk about it

- What are some of your biases about gaming?
- What are the biggest gaming battles in your home?
- What are some of the things you noticed when you played a game with your child?

LISA MONTHIE

parent of Jackson, William, and Emma, and the assistant director of instructional technology for Waco Independent School District, Waco, Texas

Early Christmas morning 2014 our son Jackson, aged 7, was over the moon when he received his shiny new Xbox One. As soon as we cleaned up, Daddy and Jackson hooked up the Xbox in the playroom. As Jackson learned how to access games (with no help from us), he began playing online with other users. We would often point out language that was inappropriate or pitch questions to all three of our children, such as, "Should you ever give out your address over the Xbox?" or "What should you do if someone asks for your phone number or username/password for your game to 'share' coins?" or "Should you talk to people on other online places separate from the Xbox?" In this way, we taught our young children how to stay safe online and enjoy gaming with people from all over the globe. We never used scare tactics but encouraged positive online presence and to be smart about what information they shared online.

Most of Jackson's games were played by children—or people who claimed they were children (this became a running joke: "Mommy, that eight-year-old sounds like he drives to school!"). There was one sweet voice that stood out to us, a girl we would later know as Abby. She and Jackson were the same age and seemed to play the same games at the same times. Abby was always positive and cautious about what information she shared. She only told us she was from Canada after months of play. Jackson and Abby would always encourage each other, and soon Jackson began calling her his friend. I would often talk to

Abby's mom in the background of the game, and sometimes we would jump in the game and just talk.

When Jackson and Abby both received iPhones for their birthdays, Jackson wanted to FaceTime and play online with Abby. We hopped on the Xbox and talked with Abby and her mom, and soon Jackson and Abby exchanged phone numbers. Playing games and FaceTime became the way they talked about all sorts of issues, from bullying to school challenges. Abby even saved up her allowance and shipped Jackson *real* maple syrup from Canada (which, if you have never had it, is the best).

Almost five years later, the games may have changed, but Jackson and Abby's friendship remains strong to this day. Jackson hopes one day to travel to Canada to visit his Canadian bestie. And it all started with an Xbox.

Cyberbullying

One of the biggest concerns we have as parents is that our child will become the victim of cyberbullying. Saying that social media is the cause of bullying is not accurate, nor is it helpful. Bullying has always existed, as has gossiping. However, when it's online it's a) in writing (so in black and white and therefore more shocking and permanent) and b) more public and more shareable.

Consider this tidbit of wisdom from sixteen-year-old Hannah Alper, who was featured in my book, *Social LEADia*. She says, "Yes, we can do bad things online, such as cyberbullying, but we can also prevent the bad things, reverse it, and do things on the internet that will help us change the world for the better." I have met so many kids who are leveraging technology and social media to make the world a better place. I learned about Konnor Suave, a student who had created a secret Instagram to compliment every student in his graduating class, and Natalie Hampton, a sixteen-year-old who had been severely bullied and who created an app called Sit with Us,[1] which allowed kids to make a plan to sit with others in the cafeteria so they didn't have to sit alone and, in many cases, could make new friends as well. I discovered Jeremiah Anthony who used Twitter to offer "sincere compliments" to others and transformed his school community as a result. At my own school, a secret account called Carter Compliments mysteriously appeared and became a source of joy for others.

When I was young, I often wondered why it is we spend so much time on messages directed to the bully, instead of creating campaigns where we focus on the victim. Today, your child can be a source of hope for someone, and all it may take is a few private messages of care and concern. When I talk with kids, I share with them that, when they encounter mean behavior online, they have a couple of choices. They can keep scrolling, they can report the comment (for every platform and app, this is completely anonymous), or they can reach out with love to the person being targeted. Their kindness could literally save a person's life (not that you would necessarily say this as you definitely don't want to put that kind of pressure on a child). Maybe your child will be the one to create a new app or club of caring pals to make a positive difference.

What Is the Relationship between Bullying and Cyberbullying?

Lots of research around cyberbullying has been done, and the results vary significantly from study to study. Part of the reason for this is how we define cyberbullying. For example, if cyberbullying is broadly defined as "anything that is posted online that's intended to hurt or upset someone else, regardless of what the topic is,"[2] then you are going to see very high numbers. But let's go back to offline behaviors: When I hear my students say out loud, "Stop bullying me," I take a second. Is this a situation of someone saying something mean and hurtful? If so, I'll say, "That is mean and hurtful, not bullying. Your language matters." I generally keep an eye on the situation to make sure it isn't a consistent behavior and will often also ask (privately) if it's a frequent and targeted behavior and check in with how the student is feeling. What I don't want to see or hear are the words bullying and cyberbullying interchanged with mean behavior. At any given time in the halls of any high school, you will hear kids being mean to each other. When I probe, they will often say they are joking, and of course, I will insist it's not funny.

Don't misunderstand me. We need to address mean behavior, but our response to mean behavior as parents is to help kids develop resiliency and strategies. When we see a mean comment online, it feels so much worse because it is in writing and permanent, but mean comments online aren't always examples of cyberbullying. Taking a device away isn't the best strategy when we are talking about mean behavior (although encouraging kids to step away is extremely beneficial). Do we take away opportunities for students to play together at recess or work in groups because they might be rude to each other? Or do we, instead, give them strategies to work cooperatively and collaboratively? Unfortunately, our kids are going to experience mean behavior in a variety of situations and contexts throughout their lives. We can't insulate them from that.

Our response to bullying has to be different. Bullying is sustained and targeted and meant to humiliate. It is about power. Believe me when I tell you I do not take the issue of bullying lightly. I know firsthand how incredibly mean people can be to those who are different. In elementary school, I was cross-eyed. I wore the wrong clothes. I allowed everyone's opinion of me to cause me to doubt my own gifts and abilities. I dreaded going to school every day, and every day I was maliciously taunted or ignored. No one physically touched me, but I felt broken nonetheless, and sometimes I wished that I was being physically assaulted because then at least I could show someone bruises and scratches and they would believe me. From time to time when I felt emboldened to tell my teacher, he would say to my classmates, "Play with Jennifer." I remember one time in particular when I got to play hide-and-seek with my classmates. I couldn't believe it. I remember feeling that that day would be the day my peers realized I was smart and interesting and worthy of befriending, only to realize that they had told my teacher what he wanted to hear, and while I spent thirty-five minutes looking for everyone, they were hiding alright—they were playing a whole other game. You can't imagine how hard it is to wake up each morning feeling so hopeless and alone. I am not proud that when I was thirteen years old, I consciously set out to take my own life. Thankfully, there were only five pills remaining in the bottle of Tylenol I took. I naively cried myself to sleep thinking I would never wake up. But I did, and I was so incredibly grateful to actually open my eyes that I never tried it again.

What would have helped me more than anything would have been for a teacher to notice and for that teacher to teach empathy and kindness to my peers. For my own parents to notice. For a caring adult to have tapped into one of my passions or strengths. For me to know someone believed in me and that just because I looked different, it didn't mean I wasn't valuable or worthy.

What was my miracle ends in tragedy for way too many kids. When I became a teacher, I made sure to teach and model empathy and multiple perspectives and to be particularly attentive to those students who might be targeted because they're different. I know all too well that our problems with bullying do not stem from social media, though they may be amplified by social media. Bullying is about cruelty, power, and apathy for other human beings. Cyberbullying can be interpreted the same way. When talking about cyberbullying, Common Sense Media uses the descriptors *intentionally* and *repeatedly*.[3]

Subtweeting, Vaguebooking, Snitchtagging, Ghosting: What Does Cyberbullying Look Like?

"Subtweeting" is a term that refers to saying something about someone without mentioning that person by name. Although the term originally referred to Twitter (tweet), it refers to the same behaviors on Snapchat, Instagram, and TikTok as well. When this is done on Facebook it is sometimes dubbed vaguebooking. The intent is age-old gossip—think *Mean Girls*. It's often mean-spirited. It is more often done by girls than boys. PG-13 examples might look like this: "When someone you thought was your friend is actually a backstabber . . ." or "People just need to mind their own business." Alternatively, it can mention someone's actual name without using the @ (mention sign) so everyone knows who you are talking about but the person you are talking about does not get a notification and may not see the comment. If you do tell the person being implicated, it is called snitchtagging.

These posts are tricky to report because they are not overtly inappropriate and do not necessarily break any app's community guidelines, but they can be very hurtful nonetheless. If your child thinks a comment is directed at them (and trust them if they think so), they may feel humiliated.

Another common problem is ghosting, which happens when someone stops responding to another person's texts or messages. I know you don't want to hear this, but some of this is normal. Your child will survive it but may need support with what to say. Consider it a win if your child shares this with you—it means that you have left the lines of communication open.

When any of these situations happen, regardless of what it's called, your child's sense of self and belonging are seriously put into question. Over the years, my kids have experienced each of these behaviors. When my daughter shared that girls she had been very close to were suddenly excluding her and saying things about her but not directed at her, my first instinct was to rush in and save the day or give advice, but truly, this is the opposite of what she needed. And believe me when I tell you that instead of helping, I infuriated her and shut down our communication. Her words ring in my ears: "Why do you always do that? I just wanted to talk about it, I don't need you to tell me what to do."

What Should I Do if My Child Is Cyberbullied?

Just like bullying, cyberbullying will impact your child's mood and behavior, as well as how they feel about themselves. Just like bullying, you want to ensure that when they share, you really listen. Your child needs to know that you love them and believe them.

Remember that most studies show that bullying still happens most frequently in person and then extends to online. Limiting phones in bedrooms will definitely help. In addition, most platforms and tools have mechanisms in place to help stop negative online behavior (though some may argue these are not stringent enough). Some of the tools you and your child need to know about are screenshot, mute, block, and report.

- Screenshot: Take a photo of what's on the screen. On some platforms (like Snapchat), the original owner will know you took a screenshot (so you may want to take a picture with another device).
- Mute: No longer see what the person is sharing (Do not Disturb on Snapchat, Snooze or Unfollow on Facebook).
- Block: You will not see what the user shares and vice versa. People are not notified they are blocked until they try to contact you.

- Report: Anonymous way to let the platform know of inappropriate use. Regularly reporting is the only way we can help create a better and safer internet.

What Will Happen if My Child Stands Up to a Bully?

I think it is important to recognize that reporting someone or standing up for what is right is a really hard thing to do. Many students shy away from doing the right thing or reporting someone or even blocking or muting someone because they are afraid of the social repercussions. These repercussions are real. I have talked to many, many students who have told me that if they stand up for someone, there is going to be a social cost to them. "The reality is, Miss [they always call me Miss], this is why we don't report." In the same way that it was really difficult for any child to walk to the vice principal's office to support me or tell on the horrible things that were happening to me, it may be just as difficult for your child to tell an adult, even a trusted one, what is going on. In-person reporting is much more difficult. Thankfully, most of the online reporting tools are anonymous.

One teacher contacted me and told me that a child in her class had reported a fake account that was created to make fun of teachers and students in the class. As a result, that child was called a snitch. They were being excluded socially, and people were being downright mean to them. The only way to stop this from happening is to circle that child with love, show them that other people do indeed make a positive difference, and remind that child of the other friends they have. Bottom line: it's complicated!

When to Worry

In a case where I failed to THINK before I posted a private message, I became the target of persistent hate messages and even death threats when a person took a screenshot of part of my message and posted it publicly. I am not going to sugarcoat this: I was definitely at risk. I felt like I was in elementary school all over again. I could not get out of bed, I couldn't eat or sleep, I couldn't focus on the simplest tasks. I felt like the whole world hated me. This situation caused me to question my own research and beliefs about the positives of social media. I was an adult with the support of a loving family and friends, and I still struggled. This experience definitely made me reflect on so much.

The strategies I suggest here are how I got through it.

1. Reflect on the message posted to begin with. Did it follow the THINK acronym? It is important for your child to recognize why the message was wrong or inappropriate and learn from it.

2. Pay particular attention to your child's behavior. Are there changes? Is your child withdrawing from normal activities? If so, the situation will require more intense action.

3. Seek out your school's administration to find out what supports they have in place or how you might work together to support your child.

4. You may need to take your child's device away for a while. This conversation can go like this: "I love you, and I believe you, and I am extremely worried about your health and well-being. I think we need help. We are going to have to take away your device for a while until we can figure this out together."

5. You may need to enlist the help of a family friend. It is healthier if both you and your child DO NOT see what

is posted. You can ask a trusted friend to only let you know if there is something you should worry about.

6. Seek a way to surround your child with another group of friends (even just one) who may or may not know about the incident and who can show love and support.

7. DO NOT respond in any way to any of the posts. This will likely only make things worse.

8. Seek organizations that can help. For example, NeedHelpNow.ca is an organization that provides help with taking down images that are posted online. BullyingCanada supports families who are dealing with bullying and cyberbullying. #ICANHELP is an organization that can provide assistance as well.

9. Talk to your family doctor and/or refer your child to a therapist or psychologist.

Above all, you need to believe your child if they tell you they are being targeted or bullied and show them you love them. Eventually, they will get through it, but they will need a whole lot of love and support. The only way to combat bullying is to create a culture of kindness and empathy. I have included a few strategies that are proven to work in the Try This! section for this chapter.

Apps to Pay Attention To

Apps that allow users to be anonymous or that allow your child to video chat with strangers—like Holla, Kik, Whisper, and Omegle—present a greater likelihood that your child may encounter negativity or even predators. You also may want to watch out for dating apps your tween has stumbled upon, such as Badoo, Bumble, Skout, or Tinder. Many of these apps have strict 18+ restrictions, but as we all know, anyone can lie about their age. If you have family sharing, you likely won't need to worry about apps like this.

Let's go back to our Media Guidelines for a second. You need to emphasize that your child should never meet in person with anyone they met online without the family knowing about it. Also emphasize that any time a picture or video leaves their phone, they can no longer control what happens to it. These apps warrant a bigger conversation as well (I am thinking Maslow): Is your child feeling like they don't belong? Are they struggling with making friends? Are they struggling with their self-esteem beyond what might be normal teenage angst?

Counteract Cyberbullying: The Science of Kindness

In her book *A Passion for Kindness*, educator Tamara Letter shares research around the impact of kindness on your brain. Oxytocin is the hormone released when you get a compliment or a hug or a "like" on that photo you posted on social media. Well, according to the Random Acts of Kindness Foundation, oxytocin is also released when you engage in giving or a random act of kindness. They also identified research that supports that kindness is linked to increased life expectancy and happiness and decreased stress, anxiety, pain, and depression. Kindness doesn't cost anything.

There is also reason to believe that kindness really is contagious. In a 2019 study, researchers Sparks, Fessler, and Holbrook showed some participants a video of a person helping his neighbors, while others were shown a video of a person doing parkour. All of the study participants were then given some money in return for taking part and told they could put as much as they wanted in an envelope for charity. (The researchers could not see whether the participants put money in or how much they put in.) People who saw the neighborly video were much more generous.[4] There is even a new institute, the Bedari Kindness Institute at UCLA, that is focused on spreading kindness and studying its impact on us.[5] I make sending thoughtful messages on a variety of platforms a regular part of my day, and I not only show my kids I am doing this, but I ensure I am send them "I Love You" GIFs or Bitmojis as well. Modeling kindness has a ripple effect!

Hugging has similar benefits. I participated in a hug-a-thon in my hometown where we set out to beat the Guinness Book of World Records for the most hugs in an hour. I went by myself. I have never hugged so many strangers in my life—full-body hugs. And although that might sound odd, it was one of the best experiences. The place pulsed with positivity. I had never really thought about the research around hugs before that day. As is seen in the science around kindness, hugging also releases oxytocin and is linked to reduced stress, fear, and anxiety.[6] I remember having this conversation after one of my parent talks and hugging several of the parents who stayed to ask additional questions, and I noted that they hugged each other as well. When my kids are having a tough time, I just body hug them— even now, when they are almost adults. There have been times when they initially push me away, but I persevere. I think the hardest thing for me about having to socially distance from my extended family was that I missed hugs. Developing a habit of kindness and hugs as a family can help when our kids are struggling socially. Modeling kindness on- and offline will help them to know that they too have the power to use their device—indeed their entire online presence— for good.

I have often seen the following quotation circulating on my Instagram feed: "It's not our job to toughen our children up to face a cruel and heartless world. It's our job to raise children who will make the world a little less cruel and heartless."

Gratitude

Regular expressions of gratitude have similar brain-boosting, mood-busting, and positive effects. My good friends Tara Martin and Tisha Richmond have a yearly month-long campaign in November called Gratitude Snaps[7] in which they encourage educators to use the fun filters in the Snapchat app to express gratitude toward people in their lives and post these beyond Snapchat. When they first launched it a few years ago, I decided that I would make online gratitude a habit. In my library, I regularly seek out kids in order to thank them or encourage them to thank others offline. Extending a habit of gratitude is an excellent way for them to demonstrate digital leadership that has benefits for both them and the receiver. Brain science supports the impact of gratitude on the release of oxytocin. Several research studies have linked gratitude interventions to positive effects on anxiety and depression.[8]

In my personal life, as well, I try to seek out one person a week to send a private message to; other times I share publicly. I will often seek opportunities to include my kids, so I am modeling an attitude of gratitude, and sometimes I will just send a Bitmoji or a gratitude Snap to my own child to remind them how much I love them. These are the habits we can begin to model when our children are quite young and continue to co-create as they get older. *Let's send Gramma an "I love you" text. Is there a more fun way to create a happy gratitude message to send?* Your child's creativity can be put to use here!

Try This! Strategies for Your Anti-Cyberbullying Toolbox

Surround yourself with positive people

One of the things I now do in a career studies class for all of the students in my school is give them a list of kids who inspire (using a Twitter list I have created), and I ask them what these kids are doing differently. It is fascinating to hear them and their conversations. The reality is kids see lots of other kids and celebrities using social media for entertainment purposes, and they see lots of kids being negative, but they really don't see other kids who have started nonprofits or who are using their social media accounts to teach someone something or to make a positive difference in the world. As mentioned earlier, following positive people online gives you a completely different experience. When the global COVID-19 pandemic was happening, news outlets were constantly bombarding us with really negative information, some of it factual and some of it not so much. In that time, I noticed so many positive things crop up as well. John Krasinski started *Some Good News* as a way to break the negativity, and now CBS has taken it and made it a part of their permanent news cycle. A student at my friend's school used that idea and created an Instagram account called the Positivity Report. At any given time during those crazy months in quarantine, you could take an art lesson by Mo Willems or listen to a book narrated by Peter Reynolds or many other authors. We could visit and learn from zookeepers and museum curators. Although it was an unusual time in our history, I can assure you that when you look at the potential of the online world differently and interrupt your feed with learning and positivity, it makes a difference in how you feel.

Role-playing

I will often ask my kids to "help" me in a situation. Usually it is based on a real scenario, and sometimes I make it up or exaggerate a scenario.

Here is an example:

Someone is being mean to another person on Instagram, and it is really getting to me. I feel like I should say something to her, but I am too emotional about it right now. I heard I can mute someone and I won't see what they are sharing. Is that a thing? I wonder if I should mute her for a few days until it doesn't bother me so much and then call her. Or, I can send her a direct message and share what I am feeling. How does this sound?

Let's unpack this and why this might be helpful. In this scenario, my children get to see me working through a digital dilemma out loud with them. I explicitly share my feelings and admit that, if I am too emotional, I might make a poor decision. I invite them to share what they know about muting someone, and by "wondering," I am inviting their opinion, without directly asking for it. I have done this for many situations. Almost every time, they share about a similar situation happening to a friend, which we then talk about. Engaging in role-play has paved the way for my kids to come to me when they are struggling with their own dilemmas.

Provide an alternative narrative

What I mean by that is asking, "What else can be true?" This is a strategy a psychologist gave us when our daughter had excessive worries. A child who worries will always go to the extreme scenario in their head, but positive self-talk will bring them out of the panic they are feeling. For example, when my daughter's friend was not responding to her about something on text, my daughter's immediate response was that she was being purposely left out. When I asked, "What else can be true?" my daughter came up with the following: Maybe her phone was dead. Or maybe she wasn't allowed to be on her phone. Maybe something was going on in her family that was making her sad or distracted and she couldn't answer. This strategy takes some guidance at first, but as you continue with it, your child may come up with several other alternatives on their own.

Different friend groups

Over the past few years, my kids have been treated poorly by friends, and their friend groups have shifted. For example, when some of my daughter's friends (who had been her friends since she was quite young) decided they were going to ignore her, create group chats without her, and exclude her from activities, we had a whole lot of tears and lots of role-playing, but at the end of the day, the deterioration of these friendships still hurt and upset her, and I watched helplessly as my daughter's heart was broken over and over again. Luckily, we were able to connect her with her neighborhood friends and the friends she had made in her swim club. I could at least remind her that these other girls thought she was awesome, and it helped a little bit. It isn't always easy, especially if you work odd shifts or you can't afford to enroll your child in an activity, but it would be worthwhile to investigate low- or no-cost clubs within your school or local community so that, when a situation like this arises, there are other people in your child's life who provide that needed sense of belonging (remember Maslow's needs). When a child is struggling with friends, it is an ideal time to help (or remind your child) to follow people and accounts that are positive and supportive.

What is not helpful is lashing out in anger or frustration. That old adage about waiting twenty-four hours before we send that email? We need to impress upon our kids the same idea. It is never a good idea to vent on social media about another person or to create a fake account to put down another person. And we definitely don't want our children to be victims of this kind of behavior. Before cyberbullying ever becomes an issue you have to deal with, you want to explicitly address and preempt such behavior, and, if for some reason it happens, you need to prepare to deal with it calmly.

Online communities

I know it might sound counterintuitive, but sometimes a child who feels very different from others in their community would really benefit from connecting with others who are like-minded. One powerful video I have seen (an advertisement for Skype)[9] is about a teen with only one working arm who was able to connect with another young woman who was going through the same experiences, first through Skype, and then in person. Sarah lives in Indiana, and Paige lives in New Zealand. I cry every time! I often wonder if I would have felt less lonely as a child if I had known someone else who was also cross-eyed and experiencing the same bullying I was. Perhaps you have already had the experience of finding a Facebook group that supports parents of children with autism or ADHD or who are gay or transgender and allows parents to share struggles and strategies. Think about how it may help your own child to connect with someone who is like-minded so they recognize they are not alone.

CALM

Dr. Jennifer Kolari, family therapist and author of *Connected Parenting*, presented at a parent session organized by our local Newmarket Parent Network. Kolari shared a therapy technique that absolutely changed my world! She talked about mirroring, which, when done correctly and in conjunction with CALM[10] strategies, can diffuse a situation and support your child. I could not take notes fast enough that night, and although Kolari never really talked about devices or social media use, I have applied it to my own context: a parent of adolescents navigating social media.

Kolari emphasized that, often, when your child is opposing you or enraged or anxious, your child is trying to send the message that they are upset. Instead of listening to my daughter send that message, I jumped in to fix things. I pulled upon my adult wisdom to tell her how to deal with it, when she is (as you will recall from Chapter

1) seeking independence and figuring out how to problem solve on her own, not to mention was completely devastated because her very important peer relationships seemed to be crumbling around her. This is what I could have done instead:

C – CONNECT

You put your phone down or use your body to indicate that you are deeply listening to your child. Kolari says, "Connect before you correct."

A – AFFECT

Affect matching means that if your child looks sad, you look sad. If they look scared, you look scared. Even if you are not experiencing the same emotions, your very expression is telling them that you really understand their experience in that moment, rather than telling them how they are feeling or trying to fix the problem.

L – LISTEN

Kolari says that, in order to show your child that you are listening and that they have been heard, it is best to paraphrase, clarify, and summarize or wonder out loud.

M – MIRRORING

Show your child that you are the person who truly gets it. Kolari says that "opiates and endorphins open in the brain when you are mirroring properly."[11]

When my next child had a similar situation happen (I think seventh grade was the worst year for both of my kids!), I tried it:

"I am going to put my device away to give you my full attention because you are obviously really upset." **(C)** (sad face, frown) **(A)**

Nod as I listen. "I am hearing that your friend Anna knew that you were home but didn't invite you and told everyone that you weren't around, and then on Instagram everyone posted how much fun they were having?" **(L)**

"Aw, kid. When the person who is supposed to be your best friend isn't honest with you and betrays you, it must feel so awful and hurtful. And to top it off, watching everyone have fun on social media must feel so crummy. You didn't do anything to deserve being treated terribly. I'm not sure if something else is going on with Anna, but right now, I am sure you don't care. Is there something I can do to help?" **(M)**

Of course, we then had to navigate the actual situation, but she trusted me to role-play, and she shared more than if I had tried to jump in and fix the situation. She felt listened to. I have used this technique through break-ups and girl drama, and just between you and me, it works on my husband too!

Let's Talk about It

- Do your kids know that you love them and will help and support them no matter what they do? How do they know?
- How might you make kindness toward others a family goal?
- Think of a bullying or cyberbullying situation you know of that you could ask your kids for advice on.

OLIVIA VAN LEDTJE

Olivia Van Ledtje ("LivBit") is a twelve-year-old reader, thinker, and kids' voice believer. Using technology to inspire empathy, equity, and activism, Olivia's mission is to share messages with the world that are hopeful, kind, and true. Olivia is the creator of LivBits—short videos for kids and teachers about reading, thinking, and life. Her work has been featured internationally as a model for digital citizenship and creation by kids. She's a seasoned keynote speaker, with her own podcast, *The KidLit Show*, and the co-author of *Spark Change: Making Your Mark in a Digital World*.

Recently, Olivia was honored at Google headquarters near San Francisco with a Digital Rock Star Award as well as a #Digital4Good award for her work on LivBits. Olivia was also honored by the Princess Diana Foundation and was awarded the 2019 Diana Award for her work on LivBits. This award is given to youth making a global difference and working to promote social causes that impact communities in positive ways. Olivia looks forward to more opportunities to work with authors and organizations that share her drive to promote reading, thinking, and digital citizenship for kids, and above all, Olivia prides herself in creating "heartbeeps" (positive vibes) for the world.

Connect with Olivia on her social media accounts @thelivbits or by visiting her website: theLivBits.com.

SHELLEY BURGESS

co-author, *Lead Like a PIRATE: Make School Amazing for Your Students and Staff*, San Diego, California

When our child, Fin, was in their early part of eighth grade, my husband and I would have told you they were having their best year yet. School seemed to be going well, they had what seemed to be a nice group of friends, we thought they were happy and even thriving. So it hit us incredibly hard when we were confronted with the reality that our child was, in fact, not doing well at all. Through a series of events that occurred within a short period of time, we learned that our child had been self-harming, that they were withdrawing from the world, and that there was a very real possibility that our child might take their own life. At the same time, our child finally came out to us as gay and was able to share with us a bit about what it had been like for them trying to navigate that journey alone.

Fin had always been drawn to technology and social media. From the time our children were very little, my husband and I made the decision that we were not going to adopt a parenting policy of banning and blocking. Instead, we opted for allowing access and working together on educating our children about the pros and cons of navigating online spaces in a safe and responsible manner. I followed most of the accounts where my children were interacting at first, and seeing things they posted or conversations they engaged in gave us opportunities to talk through some of the choices they made. So for Fin, social media was a place they learned how to navigate reasonably well, and I think when they were thirteen and fourteen years old, the connections they made on social media may have contributed to saving their life.

As we and Fin were working with psychiatrists and therapists trying to get the severe depression and anxiety that consumed our child under control, Fin rarely wanted to leave the house. They had to take time off from school, which meant they were even further isolated in many ways. Despite our encouragement to join other groups, like the youth programs at our local Pride office, Fin just couldn't do it. But while they were unable to connect with other young people in person, Fin did make connections via social media. They met other teens who were working through what it meant to navigate the world as a member of the LGBTQ+ community, connecting with other youth who also suffered from depression and anxiety. I have certainly not been privy to what all of those conversations entailed, but I do know that in them they found some comfort, some strength, some connection, and some community. And they even found their first girlfriend.

While Fin's girlfriend lived across the country from us, they connected every day, and that connection was critically important for both of them. Eventually, I was able to connect with her mother, and she and I had many tearful conversations about how grateful we were that they had found each other. We even made arrangements for our children to meet in person. The first time we traveled to Florida to all meet each other was such a special moment. Watching our children give each other their first hug brought so many overwhelming emotions into our mama hearts, and in that moment, we were both so grateful they had found each other. While that relationship did not last forever, that connection with someone else who knew exactly what they were going through was something my child desperately needed at that time in their life.

While that particular relationship ended, Fin's connection with the LGBTQ+ community continued to grow. It has helped them find strength in who they are, helped them find their voice as an activist and an advocate, helped them take their first step into our local Pride office, where they now serve as a Youth Ambassador and help other youth make connections, establish community, and find strength and pride in who they are.

Fin didn't find all that with their school friends in San Diego . . . it began with them reaching out to an online social media community.

Concluding Thoughts: Now What?

I set out to write this book to answer some of the questions parents have asked me over the years. It's short because I know you don't have lots of time. Parenting, in addition to managing a house and working, is tiring and busy. Because it's short, I know I may not have answered all of your questions, or perhaps parts of this book may not support you at this particular moment in your parenting journey. This is why I have created an online space for sharing relevant and up-to-date resources.

My hope is to start a conversation with you that isn't based on an unrealistic expectation to ditch your devices. The fact is, more and more, the internet will take over, and your dinnertime stress won't be about leaving a device in a bin at the front door because that device will be woven into your child's shirt or, as is already the case, worn on their wrist.

My hope is to encourage you to have conversations with others. Perhaps you can lend your copy of this book to another parent or create an opportunity for parents in your own community to come together to share strategies, struggles, and some of the positives.

My hope is that what I've written here has resonated and is of use to you in your parenting journey. Above all, my hope is that I have challenged you to think more critically about the headlines that often accompany stories about kids and technology. The world looks different, and that can be scary, and truth be told, there are things to fear. We should not be afraid to take what's best from our own childhood—perhaps it's a love of science experiments or fossils or hockey or scavenger hunts— and introduce our passions and interests to our own children.

Then we can also take what is completely awesome about our tech-rich lives and bring that wonder to our children as well. We can meet people from faraway lands without ever having to move out of our living rooms. We can connect with positive people and ideas that can enrich our lives and the lives of our children. We can understand that the apps, games, and social media we consume are constructed in such a way as to keep us coming back for more. We can encourage our children to lead in online spaces in ways that give them a voice they may not otherwise have. Ultimately, we can use technology to amplify our relationship with our kids, rather than destroy it.

Kids these days, your kids, are awesome, and you, in your quest to love your kids, keep them safe, and provide opportunities for them, are awesome too. We will fail sometimes, but rather than sit in the guilt or the failure, we move on, without judgment, to try again. After all, there is no such thing as a perfect parent or a perfect child.

Good luck and stay in touch,
Jennifer

Chapter resources:

jcasatodd.com → Raising Digital Leaders

Instagram for tips and conversation starters:

@RaisingDigitalLeaders

Facebook page for updated articles:

facebook.com/socialLEADia

Private Facebook group:

facebook.com/groups/raisingdigitalleaders

or scan this QR code

Endnotes

Chapter 1

1   William L. Patty and Louise S. Johnson, *Personality and Adjustment,* New York: McGraw-Hill, 1953.

2   Xianui Wang and Wanlui Xing, "Exploring the Influence of Parental Involvement and Socioeconomic Status on Teen Digital Citizenship: A Path Modeling Approach," *Journal of Educational Technology & Society* 21 (2018): 194.

3   Henry Jenkins, "Supporting Youth Participation Online," interview with Ian O'Byrne and Kristen Hawley Turner, *The Technopanic Podcast*, October 30, 2019, screentime.me/supporting-youth-participation-online/#t=1491.

4   Julie Randles, "Mash-Up 101: Let Students Practice Creativity," ISTE blog, June 23, 2018, iste.org/explore/Professional-development/Mash-up-101%3A-Let-students-practice-creativity.

5   Andy Horvath, "How Does Technology Affect Our Brains," *Voice* 11, no. 6 (2015), mdhs.unimelb.edu.au/news-and-events/news-archive/how-does-technology-affect-our-brains.

6   Lauren Sharkey, "How the Online World Is Affecting the Human Brain," *Medical News Today*, June 14, 2019, medicalnewstoday.com/articles/325461.php#3.

7   Horvath, "How Does Technology Affect Our Brains," mdhs.unimelb.edu.au/news-and-events/news-archive/how-does-technology-affect-our-brains.

8   Marie-José Harbec and Linda S. Pagani, "Associations between Early Family Meal Environment Quality and Later Well-being in School-Age Children," *Journal of Developmental & Behavioral Pediatrics* 39, no. 2 (2018): 136–43.

9   Henry C. Y. Ho et al., "Family Meal Practices and Well-Being in Hong Kong: The Mediating Effect of Family Communication," *Journal of Family Issues* 39, no. 16 (2018): 3835–56.

10 "52 Family Dinner Discussions," Southlake Baptist Church website, southlakebaptist.com/wp-content/uploads/52-Dinner-Discussions.pdf.

11 Genevieve Georget, gengeorget.com

Chapter 2

1   Jonas Grinevičius and Mindaugas Balčiauskas, "Dad Takes Photos of Him and His Daughter Sitting on the Couch since 2007, He Looks Better in Each One," Bored Panda, October 2019, boredpanda.com/dad-not-age-parenting-kids-alec -couros/?utm_source=google&utm_medium=organic&utm _campaign=organic.

2   Devorah Heitner, "Is Your Child Ready for a Cell Phone? Look for These Independence Milestones," *Washington Post,* December 17, 2019, washingtonpost.com/lifestyle/2019/ 12/17/is-your-child-ready-cellphone-look-these -independence-milestones/.

3   Wait Until 8th, waituntil8th.org.

4   American Academy of Pediatrics, "AAP Announces New Recommendations for Children's Media Use," October 21, 2016, healthychildren.org/English/news/Pages/ AAP-Announces-New-Recommendations-for-Childrens -Media-Use.aspx.

5   American Academy of Pediatrics, "AAP Announces New Recommendations," healthychildren.org/English/news/ Pages/AAP-Announces-New-Recommendations-for-Childr ens-Media-Use.aspx; American Academy of Pediatrics, "Media and Young Minds," *Pediatrics* 138, no. 5 (2018): pediatrics. aappublications.org/content/138/5/e20162591.

6   Caroline Knorr, "Tips and Scripts for Managing Screen Time when School Is Online," Common Sense Media, August 10, 2020, commonsensemedia.org/blog/tips-and-scripts-for -managing-screen-time-when-school-is-online-0.

7   Laurel J. Felt and Michael B. Robb, *Technology Addiction: Concern, Controversy, and Finding Balance,* San Francisco, CA: Common Sense Media, 2016, commonsensemedia.org/ sites/default/files/uploads/research/2016_csm_technology _addiction_executive_summary.pdf.

8   Alexandra Samuel, "Parents: Reject Technology Shame," *Atlantic*, November 4, 2015, theatlantic.com/technology/ archive/2015/11/why-parents-shouldnt-feel -technology-shame/414163/.

9   V. Rideout and M. B. Robb, *Social Media, Social Life: Teens Reveal Their Experiences*, San Francisco, CA: Common Sense Media, 2018.

10 Wang and Xing, "Exploring the Influence of Parental Involvement and Socioeconomic Status on Teen Digital Citizenship: A Path Modeling Approach," 186-99.

11 Sonia Livingstone, Giovanna Mascheroni, and Elisabeth Staksrud, *Developing a Framework for Researching Children's Online Risks and Opportunities in Europe*, London, UK: LSE, EU Kids Online, 2015, lse.ac.uk/media@lse/research/EUKidsOnline/EUKidsIV/PDF/TheEUKidsOnlineresearchframework.pdf.

12 Henry Jenkins, Mimi Ito, and danah boyd, *Participatory Culture in a Networked Era: A Conversation on Youth, Learning, Commerce, and Politics*, Cambridge, UK: Polity Press, 2015.

13 Angela Lashbrook, "The Case against Spying on Your Kids with Apps," OneZero, September 18, 2019, onezero.medium.com/the-case-against-spying-on-your-kids-with-apps-59760ec780e0.

14 Arup Kumar Ghosh et al., "Safety vs. Surveillance: What Children Have to Say about Mobile Apps for Parental Control," *Mathematics, Statistics and Computer Science Faculty Research and Publications* (2018), eecs.ucf.edu/~jjl/pubs/pn1838-ghoshA.pdf.

15 Jenkins, "Supporting Youth Participation Online," screentime.me/supporting-youth-participation-online/#t=1491.

16 Janell Burley Hofmann, "To My 13-Year-Old, an iPhone Contract from Your Mom, with Love," Huffington Post, December 28, 2012, huffpost.com/entry/iphone-contract-from-your-mom_b_2372493.

17 Ibid.

18 American Academy of Pediatrics, "Family Media Plan," healthychildren.org/English/media/Pages/default.aspx.

19 Samuel, "Parents: Reject Technology Shame," theatlantic.com/technology/archive/2015/11/why-parents-shouldnt-feel-technology-shame/414163/.

20 American Psychological Association, "Can the Kids Wait? Today's Youngsters May Be Able to Delay Gratification Longer Than Those of the 1960s," June 25, 2018, apa.org/news/press/releases/2018/06/delay-gratification.

21 Read Daniel's full rationale for the image here: docs.google
    .com/drawings/d/1CNcRY9lL6BobuY_cojoHQ2PZEqb4F
    _MeRpjeOZOnwRM/edit.

Chapter 3

1 Danielle d'Entremont, "Nova Scotia Teen Wins International
   Award for River Cleanup Work," *CBC News*, August 7,
   2018, cbc.ca/news/canada/nova-scotia/nova-scotia
   -teen-wins-international-award-for-river-cleanup-work
   -1.4776331.

2 Ishita Katyal, *Be Whoever You Want at Any Age*, TEDx
   Gateway, March 18, 2016, youtube.com/watch?v
   =Na9g6raGwio.

3 Wayne Dwyer, *Power of Intention Part 1. Positively Charged*,
   November 29, 2014, youtu.be/rrl-3ctJOSY.

4 "Social media," Merriam-Webster, merriam-webster.com/
   dictionary/social%20media.

5 Henry Jenkins, "Supporting Youth Participation Online,"
   interview with Ian O'Byrne and Kristen Hawley Turner, The
   Technopanic Podcast, October 30, 2019, screentime.me/
   supporting-youth-participation-online/#t=1491.

6 Department for Digital, Cultural, Media & Sport, UK
   Government, "Online Harms," white paper, February 12,
   2020, gov.uk/government/consultations/online-harms
   -white-paper/online-harms-white-paper.

7 Matthew Warren, "Abstaining from Social Media Doesn't
   Improve Well-Being, Experimental Study Finds," *Research
   Digest,* November 28, 2019, digest.bps.org.uk/2019/11/28/
   abstaining-from-social-media-doesnt-improve-well-being
   -experimental-study-finds/.

8 Royal Society for Public Health, *Status of Mind: Social Media
   and Young People's Mental Health and Wellbeing,* London:
   Royal Society for Public Health, 2017, ed4health.co.uk/wp
   -content/uploads/2018/12/RSPH-Status-of-Mind-report.pdf.

9 Common Sense Media, *Social Media, Social Life: Teens
   Reveal Their Experiences,* San Francisco: Common
   Sense Media, 2018, commonsensemedia.org/research/
   social-media-social-life-2018?j=6933610&sfmc_sub
   =167414493&l=2048712_HTML&u=115213283&mid
   =6409703&jb=72.

10 "About," YouTube webpage, youtube.com/about/.

11 Paige Cooper, "23 YouTube Statistics That Matter to Marketers in 2020," Hootsuite blog, December 17, 2019, blog.hootsuite .com/youtube-stats-marketers/.

12 Jenn Chen, "Important Instagram Stats You Need to Know for 2020," Sprout Blog, May 6, 2020, sproutsocial.com/insights/ instagram-stats/.

13 Gian Pepe, "33 Jaw-Dropping Instagram Statistics," Jumper Media, December 6, 2019, jumpermedia.co/ powerful-instagram-stats/.

14 Salman Aslam, "Snapchat by the Numbers: States, Demographics, and Fun Facts," Omnicore, February 7, 2020, omnicoreagency.com/snapchat-statistics/.

15 trueinteractive.com/why-snapchat-keeps-growing/.

16 Jeff Collins, "TikTok Introduces Family Pairing," TikTok website, April 15, 2020, newsroom.tiktok.com/en-us/ tiktok-introduces-family-pairing.

17 "20 TikTok Statistics Marketers Need to Know: TikTok Demographics & Key Data," Mediakix, June 11, 2020, mediakix.com/blog/top-tik-tok-statistics -demographics/.

18 Federal Trade Commission, "Children's Online Privacy Protection Rule," ftc.gov/enforcement/rules/rulemaking -regulatory-reform-proceedings/childrens-online-privacy -protection-rule.

19 Daryl Lindsey, "Social Media is Not Real Life, But That's Not the Problem," The Everygirl, November 5, 2015, theeverygirl. com/social-media-is-not-real-life-but-thats-not-the-problem.

20 Tyler Tarver, a YouTuber and fellow Google Innovator, shared this with me during his YouTube session in October 2019.

21 "Digital Footprint," TechTerms, updated May 26, 2014, techterms.com/definition/digital_footprint.

22 Danielle Elmers, "The Job-Search Statistics All Job Seekers Should Know," TopResume, ca.topresume.com/ career-advice/7-top-job-search-statistics.

23 Ariella Coombs and Jenna Arcand, "4 Things Recruiters Are Looking For When They Search You Online," Work It Daily, December 20, 2019, workitdaily.com/things-recruiters -looking-for-social-media.

24 "Digital Dualism," Techopedia, November 6, 2012, techopedia .com/definition/29046/digital-dualism.

25 "About Twitter's Account Suggestions," Twitter webpage, help. twitter.com/en/using-twitter/account-suggestions.

26 Counseling & Mental Health Center, *Perfectionism: A Double-Edged Sword,* Austin: University of Texas, 2008, lib.sfu.ca/system/files/28965/Perfectionism-U-of-Texas.pdf.

27 Sherril M. Stone, "Observational Learning," *Encyclopedia Britannica,* britannica.com/science/observational-learning.

28 Original source unknown.

Chapter 4

1 Rachel Kaser, "Fortnite Bests Russia and Japan to Become World's 8th Most-Populated Place," TNW, November 27, 2018, thenextweb.com/gaming/2018/11/27/fortnite-200-million-player-count/.

2 businessofapps.com/data/among-us-statistics/.

3 Melinda Wenner Moyer, "Do Video Games Trigger Aggression," *Scientific American,* October 2, 2018, scientificamerican.com/article/do-violent-video-games-trigger-aggression/.

4 Ibid.

5 "A Video Game Can Change the Brain, May Improve Empathy in Middle Schoolers," *Science Daily,* August 9, 2018, sciencedaily.com/releases/2018/08/180809175051.htm.

6 Daphne Bavelier, "Your Brain on Video Games," TED Talks, ted.com/talks/daphne_bavelier_your_brain_on_video_games/transcript?utm_campaign=tedspread&utm_medium=referral&utm_source=tedcomshare#t-1058425.

7 Child Mind Institute, "ADHD, Addiction, and Video Games: An Unsurprising Trio," October 9, 2019, childmind.org/blog/adhd-addiction-and-video-games-an-unsurprising-trio/.

8 Ibid.

9 Common Sense Media, "Could My Kid Be Addicted to Video Games?" commonsensemedia.org/screen-time/could-my-kid-be-addicted-to-video-games.

10 J. S. Aubrey, M. B. Robb, J. Bailey, and J. Bailenson, *Virtual Reality 101: What You Need to Know About Kids and VR*, San Francisco, CA: Common Sense Media, 2018.

11 Ibid.

12 Ibid., 4.

13 Stuart Dredge, "All You Need to Know about Roblox," *The Guardian,* September 28, 2019, theguardian.com/games/2019/sep/28/roblox-guide-children-gaming-platform-developer-minecraft-fortnite.

14 Ibid.

15 Herman Narula, "The Transformative Power of Video Games," TED Talks, ted.com/talks/herman_narula_the_transformative_ power_of_video_games/transcript?utm_source=twitter.com &utm_medium=social&utm_campaign=tedspread#t-597517.

16 David Molloy, "How Playing Video Games Could Get You a Better Job," *BBC,* August 30, 2019, bbc.com/news/ business-49317440.

17 Ibid.

18 *Social LEADia*, 90.

19 Hilary Russ, "Global Esports Revenues to Top $1 Billion in 2019: Report," *Reuters,* February 12, 2019, reuters.com/ article/us-videogames-outlook/global-esports-revenues-to -top-1-billion-in-2019-report-idUSKCN1Q11XY.

20 A. J. Willingham, "What is eSports? A Look at an Explosive Billion-Dollar Industry," *CNN,* August 27, 2018, cnn. com/2018/08/27/us/esports-what-is-video-game -professional-league-madden-trnd/index.html.

21 Russ, "Global Esports Revenues to Top $1 Billion in 2019: Report."

22 C. Steinkuehler, "Esports Research: Critical, Empirical, and Historical Studies of Competitive Videogame Play," *Games and Culture* 15, no. 1 (2020): 3–8.

23 Dom Sacco, "Let's Talk about Mental Health in Esports: 10 Individuals Share Their Stories," *ENUK,* May 14, 2017, esports-news.co.uk/2017/05/14/esports-mental -health-experiences/.

Chapter 5

1 Elyse Wanshel, "Teen Makes 'Sit With Us' App That Helps Students Find Lunch Buddies," HuffPost Canada, November 16, 2016, huffingtonpost.ca/entry/teen-creates-app-sit -with-us-open-welcoming-tables-lunch-bullying_us _57c5802ee4b09cd22d926463?ri18n=true&guccounter =1&guce_referrer=aHR0cHM6Ly93d3cuZ29vZ2xlLmNvbS8 &guce_referrer_sig=AQAAANiEU-Wg2GpjtlRowam9dACLQL qBkS_cGjQ_HdyEhECD3hj9gw45w2Xsyppm_DQnub9tqays GQ2QaJ_lgogGfz5-Xl6o3mNHY9rkFLmte2kClZ8gTT4.

2 Anya Skrba, "Cyberbullying Statistics, Facts, and Trends (2020)," FirstSiteGuide, May 2, 2020, firstsiteguide.com/ cyberbullying-stats/.

3   Common Sense Media, "What Is Cyberbullying," commonsensemedia.org/cyberbullying/what-is-cyberbullying.

4   Adam M. Sparks et al., "Elevation, an Emotion for Prosocial Contagion, Is Experienced More Strongly by Those with Greater Expectations of the Cooperativeness of Others," *PlosOne* 14, no. 12 (2019): e0226071.

5   Annie Lowrey, "America's Epidemic of Unkindness," *The Atlantic,* November 28, 2019, theatlantic.com/ideas/archive/2019/11/how-be-kind/602488/.

6   Erica Cirino, "What Are the Medical Benefits of Hugging?" Healthline, healthline.com/health/hugging-benefits#1.

7   "Gratitude Snaps," Tara Martin personal webpage, tarammartin.com/gratitudesnaps/.

8   Camille Preston, "The Neurobiology of Expressing Gratitude," *Psychology Today,* November 20, 2019, psychologytoday.com/ca/blog/mental-health-in-the-workplace/201911/the-neurobiology-expressing-gratitude.

9   "Paige and Sarah, Two Girls, Each with One Arm, Become Best Friends through Skype," Huffington Post, November 5, 2013, huffpost.com/entry/skype-paige-sarah_n_4218922.

10 "Connect with Your Kids Using the CALM Technique," CBC, January 16, 2015, cbc.ca/stevenandchris/life/the-calm-technique.

11 TVOParents, "What Is the Mirroring Technique," youtube.com/watch?v=gAsC43xongc.

Acknowledgments

Thank you to all of the digital leaders and parents who contributed their experiences to this book. Your experiences have made it so much richer. I am thrilled to shine a light on you and amplify your voices.

Thank you to Merve Lapus for his thoughtful foreword and for the work he continues to do at Common Sense Media to support educators, parents, and students.

Thank you to Dave and Shelley for believing in me and this project. Thanks to the incredible editing team and all who helped make this book a reality.

Thank you to friends and peers who read the book, provided endorsements, and supported and encouraged me along the way. In particular, Darlene, Kate, Karen, Lisa, Mandy, Tisha, Rodney, Rachelle, Katie, Annick, Tamara, and my Edumatch and #OGC online families.

Thank you for listening to me rant and always being there when I needed you.

Thank you to all of the parents who have come to listen to me speak or who have read my blog and have had the courage to ask questions. We are better when we share and learn from one another.

And most of all, thank you to my family: Stewart, Sydney, Kelsey, and my extended family—my parents and sisters and in-laws—who support me and love me and listen to me and without whom I couldn't possibly have written another book.

About the Author

Jennifer Casa-Todd is a wife, mom, teacher-librarian, and former literacy consultant. Jennifer holds a master's degree in education and digital technologies from Ontario Tech University, where she specialized in social media and digital citizenship. She is a Google Certified Teacher and Innovator, an Ontario Google Educator group leader, an executive member of the International Society Technology and Education (ISTE) Librarian PLN, a Raspberry Pi Certified Educator, and the cofounder of the Global Education Student Chat. She is the 2020 recipient of the ISTE Digital Citizenship PLN Award. Jennifer is also the author of the book *Social LEADia: Moving Students from Digital Citizenship to Digital Leadership* and coauthor of the children's book *Aubrey Bright in Stories That Connect Us*, a story about the intergenerational power of technology. Jennifer is an international keynote speaker who is passionate about showing teachers and students how they can use technology and social media to make the world a better place.

SPEAKING

Jennifer is passionate about leading and sharing beyond the walls of her school. She brings leadership, research, and practical examples and experiences to her talks. She has had the privilege of speaking to audiences from twenty to two thousand in various capacities and in various cities across Canada and the US, as well as virtually around the world.

> "We have now used Jennifer twice to coach Halton parents around the right ways to effectively parent through the positives and negatives of social media. Her ability to seamlessly connect with the audience as a fellow parent while also sharing her expertise as an educator and author strikes the perfect balance that is both engaging and informative. We will not hesitate to use her again!"
>
> **—Scott Podrebarac,** Superintendent of education, Safe and Accepting Schools, Halton District School Board

Parent Talk: Raising Digital Leaders

Parenting today is impacted by the reality that technology and social media are a part of our world. What should have us worried? What is a normal part of adolescence? How much tech is too much tech?

In this talk, Jennifer will share proactive and practical research-based strategies to help you balance tech, keep your kids safe, and support your child in using technology and social media for their future and to make a positive difference.

Additional testimonials and contact information can be found at **jcasatodd.com**.

More from

Dave Burgess
Consulting, Inc.

Since 2012, DBCI has published books that i0nspire and equip educators to be their best. For more information on our titles or to purchase bulk orders for your school, district, or book study, visit **DaveBurgessConsulting.com/DBCIbooks**.

More Technology & Tools

50 Things You Can Do with Google Classroom by Alice Keeler and Libbi Miller

50 Things to Go Further with Google Classroom by Alice Keeler and Libbi Miller

140 Twitter Tips for Educators by Brad Currie, Billy Krakower, and Scott Rocco

Block Breaker by Brian Aspinall

Building Blocks for Tiny Techies by Jamila "Mia" Leonard

Code Breaker by Brian Aspinall

The Complete EdTech Coach by Katherine Goyette and Adam Juarez

Control Alt Achieve by Eric Curts

The Esports Education Playbook by Chris Aviles, Steve Isaacs, Christine Lion-Bailey, and Jesse Lubinsky

Google Apps for Littles by Christine Pinto and Alice Keeler

Master the Media by Julie Smith

Reality Bytes by Christine Lion-Bailey, Jesse Lubinsky, and Micah Shippee, PhD

Sail the 7 Cs with Microsoft Education by Becky Keene and Kathi Kersznowski

Shake Up Learning by Kasey Bell

Social LEADia by Jennifer Casa-Todd

Stepping Up to Google Classroom by Alice Keeler and
Kimberly Mattina

Teaching Math with Google Apps by Alice Keeler and
Diana Herrington

Teachingland by Amanda Fox and Mary Ellen Weeks

Like a PIRATE™ Series

Teach Like a PIRATE by Dave Burgess

eXPlore Like a PIRATE by Michael Matera

Learn Like a PIRATE by Paul Solarz

Play Like a PIRATE by Quinn Rollins

Run Like a PIRATE by Adam Welcome

Tech Like a PIRATE by Matt Miller

Lead Like a PIRATE™ Series

Lead Like a PIRATE by Shelley Burgess and Beth Houf

Balance Like a PIRATE by Jessica Cabeen, Jessica Johnson, and
Sarah Johnson

Lead beyond Your Title by Nili Bartley

Lead with Appreciation by Amber Teamann and Melinda Miller

Lead with Culture by Jay Billy

Lead with Instructional Rounds by Vicki Wilson

Lead with Literacy by Mandy Ellis

Leadership & School Culture

Beyond the Surface of Restorative Practices by Marisol Rerucha

Choosing to See by Pamela Seda and Kyndall Brown

Culturize by Jimmy Casas

Escaping the School Leader's Dunk Tank by Rebecca Coda and
Rick Jetter

Fight Song by Kim Bearden

From Teacher to Leader by Starr Sackstein

If the Dance Floor Is Empty, Change the Song by Joe Clark

The Innovator's Mindset by George Couros

It's OK to Say "They" by Christy Whittlesey

Kids Deserve It! by Todd Nesloney and Adam Welcome

Let Them Speak by Rebecca Coda and Rick Jetter

The Limitless School by Abe Hege and Adam Dovico

Live Your Excellence by Jimmy Casas

Next-Level Teaching by Jonathan Alsheimer

The Pepper Effect by Sean Gaillard

Principaled by Kate Barker, Kourtney Ferrua, and
    Rachael George

The Principled Principal by Jeffrey Zoul and Anthony McConnell

Relentless by Hamish Brewer

The Secret Solution by Todd Whitaker, Sam Miller, and
    Ryan Donlan

Start. Right. Now. by Todd Whitaker, Jeffrey Zoul, and
    Jimmy Casas

Stop. Right. Now. by Jimmy Casas and Jeffrey Zoul

Teachers Deserve It by Rae Hughart and Adam Welcome

Teach Your Class Off by CJ Reynolds

They Call Me "Mr. De" by Frank DeAngelis

Thrive through the Five by Jill M. Siler

Unmapped Potential by Julie Hasson and Missy Lennard

When Kids Lead by Todd Nesloney and Adam Dovico

Word Shift by Joy Kirr

Your School Rocks by Ryan McLane and Eric Lowe

Teaching Methods & Materials

All 4s and 5s by Andrew Sharos

Boredom Busters by Katie Powell

The Classroom Chef by John Stevens and Matt Vaudrey

The Collaborative Classroom by Trevor Muir

Copyrighteous by Diana Gill

CREATE by Bethany J. Petty

Ditch That Homework by Matt Miller and Alice Keeler

Ditch That Textbook by Matt Miller

Don't Ditch That Tech by Matt Miller, Nate Ridgway, and
   Angelia Ridgway

EDrenaline Rush by John Meehan

Educated by Design by Michael Cohen, The Tech Rabbi

The EduProtocol Field Guide by Marlena Hebern and Jon Corippo

The EduProtocol Field Guide: Book 2 by Marlena Hebern and
   Jon Corippo

The EduProtocol Field Guide: Math Edition by Lisa Nowakowski
   and Jeremiah Ruesch

Game On? Brain On! by Lindsay Portnoy, PhD

Innovating Play by Jessica LaBar-Twomy and Christine Pinto

Instant Relevance by Denis Sheeran

LAUNCH by John Spencer and A.J. Juliani

Make Learning MAGICAL by Tisha Richmond

Pass the Baton by Kathryn Finch and Theresa Hoover

Project-Based Learning Anywhere by Lori Elliott

Pure Genius by Don Wettrick

The Revolution by Darren Ellwein and Derek McCoy

Shift This! by Joy Kirr

Skyrocket Your Teacher Coaching by Michael Cary Sonbert

Spark Learning by Ramsey Musallam

Sparks in the Dark by Travis Crowder and Todd Nesloney

Table Talk Math by John Stevens

Unpack Your Impact by Naomi O'Brien and LaNesha Tabb

The Wild Card by Hope and Wade King

The Writing on the Classroom Wall by Steve Wyborney

You Are Poetry by Mike Johnston

Inspiration, Professional Growth & Personal Development

Be REAL by Tara Martin

Be the One for Kids by Ryan Sheehy

The Coach ADVenture by Amy Illingworth

Creatively Productive by Lisa Johnson

Educational Eye Exam by Alicia Ray

The EduNinja Mindset by Jennifer Burdis

Empower Our Girls by Lynmara Colón and Adam Welcome

Finding Lifelines by Andrew Grieve and Andrew Sharos

The Four O'Clock Faculty by Rich Czyz

How Much Water Do We Have? by Pete and Kris Nunweiler

P Is for Pirate by Dave and Shelley Burgess

A Passion for Kindness by Tamara Letter

The Path to Serendipity by Allyson Apsey

Sanctuaries by Dan Tricarico

Saving Sycamore by Molly B. Hudgens

The SECRET SAUCE by Rich Czyz

Shattering the Perfect Teacher Myth by Aaron Hogan

Stories from Webb by Todd Nesloney

Talk to Me by Kim Bearden

Teach Better by Chad Ostrowski, Tiffany Ott, Rae Hughart, and Jeff Gargas

Teach Me, Teacher by Jacob Chastain

Teach, Play, Learn! by Adam Peterson

The Teachers of Oz by Herbie Raad and Nathan Lang-Raad

TeamMakers by Laura Robb and Evan Robb

Through the Lens of Serendipity by Allyson Apsey

The Zen Teacher by Dan Tricarico

Children's Books

Beyond Us by Aaron Polansky

Cannonball In by Tara Martin

Dolphins in Trees by Aaron Polansky

I Want to Be a Lot by Ashley Savage

The Princes of Serendip by Allyson Apsey

Ride with Emilio by Richard Nares

The Wild Card Kids by Hope and Wade King

Zom-Be a Design Thinker by Amanda Fox